Playful PARTNERSHIP

For Beloveds in Business

A Wise Man's Guide to Keep Harmony at Work & Passion at Play

TAYLORE ASHLIE

LoveYourLife

LoveYourLife

Love Your Life Publishing
7127 Mexico Road Suite 121
St. Peters, MO 63346
www.loveyourlifepublishing.com

ISBN: 978-1-934509-28-9
Library of Congress Control Number: 2011933962

Printed in the United States of America
First Printing 2011

Author Contact:
www.theplayfulpartnership.com
info@theplayfulpartnership.com
Cover and internal design: www.Cyanotype.ca
Author Photo by Sabine Messner: www.EnlightenedBranding.com

DEDICATION:

I dedicate this book to the beautiful men who have graced my life with their presence and who hold a Sacred Space in my heart, and to the beloved who I have yet to cross paths with, and the blissful connection we'll share.

ACKNOWLEDGEMENTS

This book would not exist if it were not for the contributions of some very special people. The first person I wish to acknowledge is my incredible business partner and dear friend, Howard Copeland, who I more lovingly refer to as my Angel. It is because of his faith in me, and his unwavering support as business partner and friend that I have been able to take the time to write this book, develop the highest quality coaching service, and receive the quality work of my brilliant publisher, Lynne Klippel. Thank you Howard, for your continued faith, support and friendship, and for being my surrogate dad/ uncle and my beloved friend. You are a beautiful example of the Divine Masculine.

I acknowledge Lynne Klippel, for her brilliance, support, coaching and expert guidance. Lynne you are the best of the best. I am honored and blessed to you have you publish my work.

I am in deep gratitude to T. Harv Eker for the kindness he showed me the first time we spoke, and for recognizing me as a diamond in the rough as he took a chance and put me on his stage for the first time back in 2003. It is thanks to Harv that my speaking and facilitation career was birthed. The time I spend facilitating at T. Harv Eker's event is still one of my favorite times of the year. Thank you, Harv, for the contribution you have made to my life and the lives of so many others.

I acknowledge my mentor Kendall Summerhawk and her Divine Masculine husband, Richard Shapiro for the contribution they have made to me becoming the skillful coach that I am today. Thank you for your brilliance. I have been officially Kendallized!

I acknowledge Jeffrey Armstrong who taught me so many layers and the full truth of living a Tantric lifestyle. I thank you, Jeffrey, for sharing your dedicated knowledge and wisdom on the Vedic teachings and the contribution it has made to both my personal and professional life. I acknowledge Sandi Graham, Jeffrey's beloved for the graciousness of her hospitality during the many visits I made to their beautiful home. I thank you both for the magnificent role models you both play as Divine Beloveds in Business.

I express my deepest gratitude to my sister friend, mentor and the ultimate High Priestess, Anyaa McAndrew for her loving guidance as she facilitated myself and my dear sisters of my Priestess circle, and Magdalene circle through the most transformational 18 months of my life. The Shamanic Priestess process and the Magdalene process was a powerful deep journey that I will cherish for life. It has stripped away all that was still an illusion in my life and guided me to step into my truth and authenticity as a woman in the most beautiful way. It is because of the Priestess process and my ordination into the Madonna Ministry that I am able to powerfully serve in and be a guide for other women to help them step into their authenticity and truth as the Divine Feminine beings that they are. Thank you Anyaa. I love you Sistar!

I acknowledge and thank Baba Dez Nichols for his gifted guidance, and for his ability to introduce me to my inner Divine Masculine self in the most profound and powerful way. Thank you Dez for the transformation this contributed to the quality of my healing work, and the positive shift it created in my life.

I honor and express my love to my mother Marie, my stepfather Ian and my sister Megan. Thank you for being my family and for your unconditional love. I acknowledge Tim my brother, and wish for him peace and happiness in this life. I acknowledge my half brothers Tommy and Deano as the fine men that you are. I'm sure our paths will cross again some day.

Last but not least, I express my love and appreciation for the many amazing Sister friends I am blessed with in this lifetime. It is thanks to you that I am the woman I am today. It is thanks to you that I can lead other women with confidence, grace and humility. I will always cherish the moments we dance together like no one is watching.

TOGETHER

It is our nature to need and give love, to long for touch and passion,
To have someone who's part of us to share our joy and sorrow.
People come in and out of our lives; some stay a moment, some for a lifetime.
How long we will share the same path together, this we can never know.
The key to happiness in relationships is to cherish them while they last.
Allow complete freedom for each to evolve in the highest way for them.
Always place your friendship first in hand with trust and respect.
Leave fear and resentment in the past, move on without expectation.
If you still suffer from a loss, the pain will stop when the clinging ceases.
As we mature, we each acquire habits that become our nature.
You can't change the other so accept their flaws, then take a look in the mirror,
See all the things they must live with as well, and be one another's teacher.
When the harmony and balance is right, you can feel the ease and comfort.
If tension builds, communicate; release it with love and compassion.
The journey may be a challenge at times, but the rewards are worth the effort.
Cherish the moments of love and laughter and savor the joy and passion.

- TAYLORE ASHLIE

The wolf is a symbol of loyalty and mates for life.
Illustration by Taylore Ashlie

ABOUT THE AUTHOR

This book is a collection of the wisdom and knowledge I have gained along my journey as facilitator, speaker, entrepreneur, healer, spiritual advisor, intimacy coach, Tantric student and guide, friend and lover. My desire is to help others to live with greater ease, remember how magnificent they are, experience more calm, bliss, play and abundance.

I was born and raised in Halifax, Nova Scotia, and moved to Toronto in my late twenties. There I worked as a professional magician for several years. My performance career then evolved to an acting career while selling my hand crafted items, and illustrated poetry on the side. Woven through all of this was my continuous journey of spiritual exploration, sexual healing and my foundation as an energy healer and teacher.

After moving to Vancouver in 2001, I discovered the work of T. Harv Eker, by attending his Millionaire Mind Intensive at Peak Potentials Training. It created a powerful shift in my life. I was also intrigued as I observed the facilitators on stage and knew this was work I wanted to do. I knew I had something unique to offer, and to my good fortune, when I approached Harv about it, he saw something in me as well. He contracted me to facilitate at one of his events the following summer and I've been there ever since. It was through my work at Peak Potentials that my facilitation and coaching career blossomed. I love to share my knowledge, experience and healing abilities, while weaving in a bit of playfulness, with the intention of reminding others that life is supposed to be fun. Now it is my privilege to share the same through my writing.

I have been self employed for most of my adult life. I have created a successful career on and off line as a coach, healer and speaker. I understand the challenges involved with running a small business and appreciate the freedom which comes with it. I've studied marketing from the best. Through my gift of teaching, I love to share my knowledge and wisdom with my clients and support them toward success.

I have facilitated thousands of participants in workshops on how to find their sense of calm amidst chaos. In private sessions, I have coached hundreds of men and women, but especially men, on finding greater balance, inner peace, passion, and a deeper connection within themselves and their relationships.

My favorite sessions have been those with couples. I consider it a great honor to witness two people who love one another go through a transformation which results in greater harmony, a deeper connection and adds blissful heat to their relationship. My training and experience as an ordained Minister, Shamanic High Priestess, and my Tantric lifestyle, has enriched my ability to show up in a greater way for myself and for my clients in all aspects of my work.

I am an energy specialist. I can feel the energy in any situation. I help others see how to adjust that which is out of alignment, and bring it back into alignment. In doing so, they feel more connected to Source, and have greater clarity and a sense of calm on how to move forward in their business and within their relationships.

"I think of life itself, now, as a wonderful play that I've written myself...And so my purpose is to have as much fun playing my part."

- SHIRLEY MCLAINE

CONTENTS

INTRODUCTION

Being partners in both business and love creates a whole realm unique unto itself. It can be a truly rewarding journey or it can end up creating unnecessary power struggles, destroying what you cherish the most and have worked so hard to find and create.

It's an exciting journey as you venture into a new business with your beloved. The passion you feel for one another is now coupled with a new passion as you nurture your business and grow it together to create the life you've dreamed of. Perhaps you each have your own separate businesses. In that case both businesses still exist in the same household. So there you are, two entrepreneurs living together, weaving your businesses together, and being one another's support system. Either way, you are in business with your beloved. It requires your full attention to yield success, and it's easy to get caught up in the adrenaline rush that comes with the creative process or landing that next client.

It can be challenging enough to turn off business thoughts when you are a solo entrepreneur. When you're a couple in business, and feeding off one another, you may find yourselves living and breathing the business. All too soon you may find yourselves bringing the boardroom into the bedroom. When this becomes a consistent practice, death to passionate playtime results. Running the business can also leave you too exhausted or preoccupied to even think about sexual intimacy. Falling into this pattern is very unhealthy. It can take its toll on your physical, mental, emotional, and spiritual well being. If left to wander in this direction for too long, it can even lead to infidelity or the demise of your relationship.

What I do is to raise awareness about the core differences of how men and women think, feel, and behave in business and in regard to sex. I show how the dynamics of this can create problems and conflict in your professional and personal relationship. I then share how you can use these differences to your advantage so that they enhance and contribute to your relationship and business, rather than tear it apart. I also teach communication techniques, ensuring that both partners feel fully seen and heard. I demonstrate how to effectively shift gears, so playtime can exist and the business can thrive.

In this book you will discover how to create an even deeper connection than the one you already have, and even how to reactivate a lost connection. You will also learn secrets to help your woman open up to you more completely in passionate love, and to how to experience a hotter, juicier sex life. You will discover how to use the power of this love and passion to send your business soaring to success.

I am qualified to teach these life lessons because I have lived them, done the research, and applied them. I have witnessed incredible transformations in people's lives and relationships through my work. At age 55, I am professionally focused and my spark for romance and intimacy is alive, vibrant, and stokes a fire within me that continues to enhance and energize all areas of my life. If this sounds like an existence you would like to experience with your beloved, read on!

We women can be the most confusing and frustrating beings you will ever have to deal with. I get that. We can also be a pathway to pure bliss. As you come to a better understanding of those aspects of us that drive you crazy, you will achieve greater clarity of thought regarding what to do (or not to do), and how to communicate more effectively with your beloved. She may still drive you crazy, but you'll have more fun with it. You'll know how to be her hero and the man who inspires her to be the partner and lover of your dreams.

The contents of this book are my own opinions, feelings, and viewpoints. I can only speak from my perspective, so take what resonates with you and leave the rest. I share insights which will help peel back the layers and get to the core of some deeply rooted issues. I also offer practical "how to" tips which you can apply now to create a better balance between your professional and private lives together.

For simplicity's sake, I have chosen to write this book as if I were speaking to a man. However, it is intended for both men and women, and its benefits will be even more effective if both of you read it and apply what I share with you.

If you are single, congratulations! By the time you turn the last page of this book, you will be much better prepared for the next stage in your love life.

If you are a woman in partnership, enjoy! I am confident you will love how the following pages will enlighten and enhance your relationship with your beloved. If you would like to experience an even deeper connection with him than you already have, this book is for you. If you like the idea of savoring an even hotter, juicier, more romantic relationship than the one you already have, read on! Perhaps you've been experiencing blocks in your relationship and don't know what to do about it. This book may have the answers you have been looking for. Appling the advice in this book will lead to consistent harmony in your communication with one another, both in your business and your personal relationship. It will be a guide to help you feel fully seen, heard and cherished by your beloved. So enjoy reading this book, and get it into the hands of your beloved as well!

My wish is that that my words will enlighten, inspire, and help create a deeper awareness, a spiritual connection, a hot juicy passion and abundance in all areas of your lives together. All work and no play is just not a fun existence. Couples in a playful partnership know how to have fun in business and experience bliss at home. Sometimes we're just so close to our own stuff, such as our thoughts, emotions and the challenges we are trying to work through, that we can't see how to make things flow the way we want. I am confident that, as you put my words into action, you will continue to create a fulfilling and passionate life together on all levels, one that leaves others looking on with awe.

The Playful PARTNERSHIP

"As long as life continues, the creative challenge is to tussle, play, and make love with the present moment while giving your unique gift."
- David Dieda, "The Way of the Superior Man"

PART ONE:
THE FOUNDATION

"After God created the world, he made man and woman.
Then to keep the whole thing from collapsing, He invented humor."
- Bill Kelly; screenwriter

The Dance *of the* Masculine *and* Feminine

The masculine and feminine are two very different ways of being, both in business and in love. What works in business can kill the romance in a relationship. Struggles and conflicts often result when couples don't understand the consequences of their energy balances being thrown out of whack. As long as couples continue in this direction their relationship will develop a dynamic which makes it impossible to fire up intimacy. The clients I receive in my private sessions are often suffering from stress and exhaustion from over work. They come to me to let go, clear their minds, and learn how to be more "in the moment" with their partner. I provide coaching to help them understand the dynamics of the energy they resonate, and to determine whether it contributes to or contaminates their relationship.

I will be referring to the masculine and feminine essences throughout this book. When I refer to a woman being in her masculine essence, I'm not talking about her being a tomboy or having a masculine edge. Rather I am referring to an actual form of energy; by "essence" I'm talking about the qualities which are expressed through masculine or feminine energy and to what degree we are each expressing either one. A man can be very connected to his feminine essence and still have a masculine presence.

The four aspects to our human existence are the physical, mental, emotional and spiritual. The physical and mental are qualities of the masculine. The emotional and spiritual are qualities of the feminine. Feminine energy is all about flow and movement. You've surely noticed that a woman who is naturally very feminine can be beautiful to watch as she gracefully moves her body. Emotions are in constant fluid motion. Focus, direction, decision-making, control, and confidence are all qualities of masculine energy and more structured.

We are more than just humans, however. We are human beings. As beings, we are extensions of Source energy. Divine Feminine is the feminine aspect of God Source, also referred to as Goddess. It is the energy of love, compassion, nurturing, inspiration, intuition, and creative expression. So, whether we are male or female, our ability to express these energies is determined by how connected we are with our inner Divine Feminine.

The Divine Masculine is the masculine aspect of God source. It is the energy of witnessing without judgment, providing safety, holding space and guidance. So when we are aligned with our inner Divine Masculine, whether we are male or female, we are embodying the Healthy Masculine, as we witness without passing judgment and we provide a sense of safety within ourselves and among those around us.

There are layers to this masculine/feminine dance. For example: a man can be very masculine in nature and in the way he stays focused and in control. However, if he is disconnected from his Divine Masculine self, a woman will not feel safe in his presence. At the same time, if he is disconnected from his Divine Feminine self, he cannot express love. A woman can be very feminine in nature, such as in the way she gracefully moves across a dance floor. However, if she is disconnected from her Divine Feminine self, she can come across as cold and uncaring. If she is disconnected from her Divine Masculine self, she will be very judgmental, first toward herself, then she will project it upon others. See the connection? Connecting with our masculine and feminine energy is one thing. Connecting to our Divine Masculine and Divine Feminine essence is the whole package. It is what makes it easier to live with ourselves and one another.

The motivating force behind a woman's existence is love: giving love, receiving love, feeling deeply loved, or experiencing love. The part of a woman which is feminine will either open in loving surrender to you or close to you in what will become an emotional test of your ability to open her up to you. The motivating force to a man's existence is freedom. Yes, love is high on his list too, but freedom more so. I know this resonates with you. A man must feel free to hold on to his vision and pursue it, or he weakens and cheats himself and his woman of his authentic self.

Our masculine and feminine energies fluctuate depending on the circumstances. In his book, *The Way of the Superior Man*, David Dieda shares that, in about 80% of couples, the man carries a masculine sexual essence and the woman carries a feminine sexual essence. I will be primarily speaking to that 80% of couples throughout the book. About 10% of couples are more neutral or balanced, and in the other 10%, the man carries a more feminine essence and the woman a more masculine one. For a couple to continue to enjoy a romantic sexual relationship, the polarization of the masculine and feminine must be in balance. Even same sex couples need this balance of polarity for sexual intimacy to flow. The moment one partner does something to shift further into his or her masculine or feminine while the other partner stays the same or goes in the opposite direction, sexual intimacy declines. The polarity is no longer in balance.

The degree to which you are in your masculine and feminine determines how you act, how you run your business and how you make love. A better understanding of the dynamics of the two and how they determine your behavior can save you pain and conflict, and ease you into a more harmonious existence. Running your business then becomes more fun and productive, and you gain greater skills at communicating with the opposite gender. Additionally, the intimate connection with your beloved deepens, which in turn can inspire more blissful sex in your relationship

Sometimes the difference between the masculine and feminine energy drives us crazy and makes us want to run screaming in opposite directions. And yet these same differences, viewed from a new perspective and with a dash of amusement, may become the greatest gift you can embrace in both your professional and personal lives.

In my women's workshops, I help my students become more expressive in their Divine Feminine essence. To do this, I first teach them how to connect more deeply with their inner Divine Masculine. You see, the degree to which they feel free to express their Divine Feminine self is determined by how in alignment they are with their Divine Masculine. Providing safety is a primary essence of the Healthy Masculine. When women don't feel safe, we intuitively shut down and close ourselves off for protection. As a woman creates a healthy Divine Masculine energy within herself, she feels a greater sense of self worth, confidence, and safety. The same is true with men. Lack of self worth is a result of the inner Divine Masculine not showing up, for he would never judge. The more the Divine Masculine is in place, the more the feminine feels safe and is free to flow, open up, express herself, and become more receptive.

You can be certain that those who judge others are, at their core, expressing a reflection of how they see themselves. Whenever you feel yourself becoming the target of someone else's judgment, just remember that it's not about you. You are simply the target of their projection. Deep down they are not happy about something within themselves. As humans, we're all prone to a moment of crankiness. But happy, self loving people do not continually lash out at others.

I have made myself aware of the dance between my feminine and masculine energy to the point that I am able to shift from one to the other at will. This has served me well, especially in my healing work with clients who have unhealthy father issues. By tapping into and speaking from my Healthy Masculine and reflecting to them that same form of love, I can guide these clients to connect with that same essence within themselves. As they make this connection, and feel their own Healthy Masculine energy, they learn to manifest that energy for themselves in a way that their fathers were not able to. This makes it possible to break the pattern of unhealthy father energy and to help reclaim a sense of worth. The ability to connect with my inner Divine Masculine also contributes to a deeper sense of inner calm and confidence in my own life, as well as the freedom to feel feminine, juicy, and romantic, while still allowing me to get the job done.

The three driving forces in a man's life are: hunt and kill, protect and be honored, and sex. In modern day, a man's career serves as the outlet for hunt and kill. As for protect and be honored, this is in complete alignment with qualities of the Divine Masculine. The drive for sex insures that we continue to procreate. Sex is physical and exhilarating for the man.

The woman, who you hope is expectant, is hopeful for some tenderness, appreciative talk, then arousal, then satisfaction. Women need this sequence because the feminine is emotional. Once our emotions are stimulated, it can become physical and exhilarating. At times a woman can jump straight to arousal. That depends upon the man's ability to connect and be strong in his presence. This I go into more detail in the sections titled *Presence and Ecstacy.*

Business is physical and exhilarating for the man. For it to be exhilarating for the woman, it must stimulate her emotionally and her feminine qualities of creative expression, inspiration and nurturing.

I believe the reason why traditionally men have been more successful more quickly in their business endeavors is because of their gift of single focus. Hunt and kill. That's a turn on for you. See the target, get it, close the deal. For a business to thrive, you must also make decisions, be in control, provide solid guidance to your team. These are driving forces behind any successful business and all aspects of the masculine energy.

Here's the kicker. A woman has to shift more into her masculine energy to some degree in order to run the business. She usually doesn't do this consciously. It is simply what's required to get the job done. She has to be in control of the business, be focused, and make decisions. Think about it. If you feel the romance in your relationship is slipping away, it's quite possible that this is because the shift back into her feminine essence is not taking place after business hours, and therefore the polarity required to have that juicy connection is no longer present. Even stay at home moms can fall into this pattern. Raising children requires them to be in control and make important decisions.

Fortunately, women now have access to great female coaches on the internet, who can teach them how to use their feminine strengths to promote themselves more effectively in business. Helping women market themselves and do business the Divine Feminine way is a specialty of the business coaching I provide. Until recently, most coaches on the Internet were men. The masculine method of marketing works great for the man and your single-focused self, but when women try, it often leaves us feeling exhausted and drained.

Men need the adrenaline rush to create and to prosper. When you tap into your hunt and kill instinct and aim for your target and go for it, you feel that adrenaline rush. That adrenaline rush is what makes it possible for you to create empires. If there is no adrenaline, you can't create. Dr. Ellie Drake, founder of BraveheartWomen.com, wisely refers to adrenaline as the prosperity hormone for men.

However, it is not the prosperity hormone for women. Adrenaline has the reverse affect on the feminine. It actually blocks prosperity from coming into our lives. This is not some theory, there's actually a scientific explanation. Dr. Ellie Drake explains, that when women try to get the job done the masculine way and our adrenaline is released, we become biochemically incongruent with our purpose. It triggers a fight or flight reaction, which eliminates the feeling of safety for us. Our body then becomes in conflict with our purpose and we end up fighting against ourselves. We become stressed, overwhelmed and get stuck in thoughts and feelings of lack. We also distrust our ability to get the job done. This fight or flight reaction can literally cause the feminine to shut down as a built in means of protection.

A woman's power is in her natural nurturing ability. However, in order to provide nurturing, a woman must also receive consistent nurturing. After all, you cannot give what you don't already have. The release of oxytocin is what fills a woman up with nurturing energy. When a woman breast feeds, she releases the oxytocin hormone, and it causes abundance in the form of milk. Oxytocin is also released through hugging and cuddling. It can even be released through breathing techniques and making sound.

When I do healing work on my clients, I do sound toning over their chakras to help open the energy and I encourage them to do the same. Making a "haaaaa" sound on the exhale, not in the form of a sigh, but rather through strong vocalization, can greatly sooth the feminine and actually release the oxytocin hormone. Dr. Ellie Drake refers to oxytocin as the prosperity hormone for women. She explains that adrenaline actually antagonizes oxytocin and stops it's ability to be released from our body. This is apparent when a mother breast feeds. If she is feeling anxiety, she is unable to produce breast milk. This is because anxiety releases adrenaline, and the adrenaline blocks the oxytocin, there fore the abundance of milk production is stopped.

The same is true in business. Adrenaline blocks abundance. So be careful about trying to have your woman do business your way. This is a common mistake of many masculine leaders. They see it working so well for them, so they try to teach their way to the women. Women make the same mistake. They see men having great success, so they try to model their methods and become exhausted and broke in the process.

The way a woman attracts abundance and prosperity is to release her oxytocin hormone as much as possible. She can do this by first making sure she feels nurtured first. Then she can, instill a feeling of being cared for within her clients and from the intention of being in service. The key is for her to honor these qualities as the gifts, and strengths that they are, and acknowledge the value they provide. When she does this and stands in her power by charging what she is worth and feels at peace with that, a woman can experience great financial success. The greater her financial success, the more people she can help. This cycle of abundance and greater caring is the turn on for the woman. When the opposite genders work together in a way which fully utilizes each of their driving forces, you create a business which is destined for success.

Just as women benefit from the masculine energy of focus, a man's business approach can benefit from tapping into the feminine energy of compassion. I go into more detail on this in the section titled *Focus.*

As a woman whose feminine is very dominant, it's taken a lot of effort to bring a more masculine presence into my professional life. I'm all about flow. I can flow from this to that, and dance around in my own lovely little land of flow with many different things going on at once. From a creative perspective, it works for me. In my business, however, it can lead to unfinished projects and financial struggle. The down side of our nurturing nature with regard to business is that we want to take care of everyone. I've certainly learned from experience the problem this presents. I used to try to promote to too large an audience and thus attracted too few people. Now that I have a specific niche, or tribe as I like to call it, and as I tap into my masculine energy to make and implement clear and precise decisions, things come together and move forward.

As you read on, you will discover how to be more present for your woman in such a way as to help her shift back into her feminine essence after business hours. As this takes place, you will help her open up to love.

The dance of the masculine and feminine is prevalent everywhere in nature. The balance between the two is needed to maintain balance on Planet Earth. It is very liberating and empowering for both men and women to connect with the Divine Masculine and Divine Feminine within ourselves. To do this, it helps to acknowledge that we are in fact Divine- extensions of Source energy. Acknowledging that we are eternal beings, not limited to our bodies, opens us to the possibility of a much deeper, more profound, and intimate connection. This is not about religion. It simply means being conscious that there is more to us than bones and flesh. There is our mind, of course. The brain is a beautiful computer. It stores information and keeps us safe. However, the mind should serve us, not the other way around. When we serve the mind, the ego rules our life. Who we really are is determined by how we choose to love and how we choose to deal with fear. It is our way of "being" with ourselves and one another. As you see this truth in yourself and in your partner, as you become consciously aware of the dance between the masculine and feminine, the result will be a greater sense of peace, purpose, passion, and harmony within your self, and in your relationship. Taken together all this will lead you toward the success you desire with much greater ease as well as a more playful existence.

"Intimate relationship is never the priority in a masculine man's life and always the priority in a feminine woman's life. If a man has a masculine sexual essence, then his priority is his mission, his direction toward greater release, freedom, and consciousness. If a woman has a feminine sexual essence, then her priority is the flow of love in her life, including her relationship with a man whom she can totally trust, in body, emotion, mind and spirit. Man and woman must support each other in their priorities if the relationship is going to serve them both."

- David Dieda, "The Way of the Superior Man"

"It is only when we silent the blaring sounds of our daily existence that we can finally hear the whispers of truth that life reveals to us, as it stands knocking on the doorsteps of our hearts."

- K.T. Jong

The Tantric Connection

It seems no matter how often you ask for a definition of Tantra, you'll get a different answer. Tantra is an ongoing learning process, therefore I consider myself its student. However, what I have learned up to now, I have learned from masters. It is a lifestyle for me, so I will offer as clear and as simple an explanation as I can from my perspective. Often when people hear the word Tantra, there's an assumption that it's all about sex. I understand this. If you go on the internet and Google "Tantra," you will find an abundance of information that reinforce this belief. This is very misleading and just not true.

Sacred Sexuality is a beautiful aspect of living a Tantric lifestyle. However, the Tantric lifestyle encompasses all aspects of life, including how we live with family, how we treat other people, the Earth, all living things, and even our way of *being* in business. In Sanskrit, "tan" means "breath." You could say "Tantra" means "moving toward one's breath," or more clearly, "one's truth." It is about weaving energy. The English word "tension" was derived from the word "Tantra." Imagine weaving two energies together, then stretching them as far apart as you can without breaking the connection- thus creating tension. That is Tantra. The variations on how this can be applied are endless.

I attended a gathering at the home of one of my mentors, Jeffrey Armstrong. The teaching he shared with us was spiritually and mentally stimulating. He had raised the energy level in the room so high that when it was time for a break, he requested that we remain silent. He knew that if we began to chatter, it would disrupt the energy and the tension would be broken. We could feel the beautiful tension linger in the air as we hurried back to our seats for more. That is Tantra.

I attended a musical performance by Vancouver musician, singer and voice coach, Jerry DesVoignes where I had the same experience. The music was divine. As we sang along, we could feel the vibration rising in the room. When the song was over, its energy lingered in the air. Jerry requested silence so as not to disperse the energy we had created. During that silence, we could feel the delicious tension as we anticipated the beginning of the next song, while still connected to the one just completed. That is Tantra.

The chakras are the body's energy activation points. The upper chakras are the ones which activate the connection to the spirit realm, higher vibration, and consciousness. The lower chakras are the ones which activate the connection to the physical realm. There are three primary colors of Tantra: white, red and black. The practice of black Tantra is the weaving of dark, shadow energy. The closest comparison would be that of the black arts, or voodoo. Not the type of Tantra I personally choose to take part in, and not one I recommend.

Red Tantra is the practice of drawing the energy downward. It focuses on the lower chakras of the power center and primal sexual energy. The first chakra is the root, located at the perineum. It is what can keep us grounded and connects us to the physical earth. This is also the chakra connected to money and our primal force. When this chakra is closed, money issues can show up. When it is disconnected from the heart greed can appear. The second chakra is the activation point for both the sexual and creative energy. When this chakra is disconnected from the heart, it can result in lust and obsession. Many who practice Red Tantra are sexually repressed or sexual addicts. It is a selfish practice. I do not say this in judgment. That's simply what is.

The practice of White Tantra involves weaving the energy of the upper chakras and activating the energy of love, compassion and Divine connection. It is a path to enlightenment and God realization. As you integrate the practice of White Tantra into your professional life and your relationship with your beloved, family, friends and self, it can only enhance and continue to improve these areas of your life. Exercises to help with this can include meditation, eye gazing, breath work and sound toning.

When we weave the practice of White Tantra with our emotional, sexual, creative and physical connection to the Earth, we are more complete as spiritual beings in these physical bodies. This is also referred to as Pink Tantra. It is the practice of Sacred Sexuality. White Tantra and Pink Tantra are what I personally practice and what I teach.

"Pink Tantra embraces both the spiritual and the sexual aspects of the practice. This is the path where the heart is opened and lovemaking is practiced with honor and reverence. It is a merging of embodied souls, for both pleasure and enlightenment."

- Baba Dez Nichols and Kamala Devi, "Sacred Sexual Healing"

A Spiritually based Tantric lifestyle includes being fully conscious and present in the moment. It is the practice of being fully aware of and savoring the energy around you, the energy which you emanate and attract. Eckart Tolle has awakened millions of people through his talks and writings on this subject and on the power of Now. The key is to be aware of how your Now affects your next moment. Most teachings out there on the Law of Attraction are really just ways of living a spiritually aware Tantric lifestyle. This is a lifestyle in which you become fully conscious of the energy and vibration you are generating in relation to what you are receiving back. It means possessing an inner knowledge of who you are as the creator of your own reality and your connection to all things. It is about being consciously aware of how you weave the energy of the masculine and feminine into your daily lives.

White Tantra is about respecting your boundaries as well as those of others. It is a way of being. When this practice is introduced into your professional life, especially one you share with your beloved, you experience a flow in your business which will open you up to abundance on all levels; financially, spiritually, and emotionally.

Couples who fully commit to living a Tantric lifestyle learn to live and work in harmony and savor a passion and a deep connection in their love life, the kind others long to experience. There are those who live such a life without even including Tantra in their vocabulary. Through their own life experience and personal quest they have attained a conscious awareness which naturally coincides with a spiritual Tantric practice. Once you attain this knowledge you too will have a deeper understanding of the differences between the masculine and the feminine. This knowledge can greatly enhance and, in some cases, even save your business and your relationship.

Life is a more graceful journey when we keep our ego intact and are conscious of our actions. Our thoughts, daily interactions, and our lives unfold more effortlessly. It is our nature as spiritual beings to be in a constant state of expansion and exploration. Those whose lives appear to stagnate rather than expand have probably forgotten who they really are. They are caught up in the illusion that the physical plane is all that is. The truth is, it is impossible for life to be stagnant. Life is in a constant state of movement. We are either flourishing, or deteriorating. Equally important for those following a spiritual path is to remember that they also have a physical experience. I sometimes see spiritually based people struggle with an either/or mindset. They fear that the desire to make money or placing importance on physicality will make them less spiritual. This is not an either/or situation. We are spiritual beings in physical bodies. Both the physical and spiritual are at play here. They are both meaningful and play an important role in our existence. We came to this earth as spiritual beings wanting a physical experience. So play with it. As we consciously weave and explore the expansiveness of both realms while maintaining the connection of the two, we practice Tantra.

Becoming more conscious requires that we speak only in a loving manner and let go of harsh speech, especially during a conflict. That said, it's natural when feeling stressed that we snap at those we are closest to. It happens. When you do this with your partner, the time it takes you to recover, make peace, and both come back to a place of love will determine your level of consciousness. If it takes longer than a day to come back, you still have some evolving to do. If it takes a few hours, you're getting closer. When you are able to stop, take a breath, and recover immediately, then you have fully evolved in your ability to communicate with your beloved. Snapping as a reaction to stress is one thing, as long as you recover quickly. Talking down to your beloved is never acceptable.

Sharing details about your intimate sex life with anyone but your partner does not serve your relationship either. An exception would be the professional services of a trusted intimacy coach or therapist. Even in a mutually agreed polyamorous relationship, the intimacy that two partners share together in private must be kept sacred. To do otherwise would fragment the bond.

Sacred Tantric Sexuality is the integral and conscious connection of our sexuality to our spirituality. It is the acknowledgment that it is our creative force and is a gift from Divine Source. The practice of Sacred Sexuality is the practice of living in your truth as a spiritual being in a physical body. This can be explored with your partner or as a solo practice. When my clients are ready to take their intimacy and sexual connection to a deeper level, I begin where they are at that time, and meet them there. We establish boundaries and honor them. From there we can discover what problems need to be aired so they can communicate and address their needs more fully. I coach them to a place where they feel that their partner has understood them on a deeper level. I then guide them to weave their spiritual selves more deeply into their sexual experience, both within themselves and one another. I teach communication techniques which help them become more truthful and be more present for one another during intimacy. When the sexual experience becomes a spiritual experience, feeling completely devoid of guilt or shame, free to let go, fully present, and honoring yourself and your partner, you experience Divine Union.

The word "Namaste" means "I see you." This phrase is used often in the movie *Avatar*. It means, "I see who you are. I see the Divine in you." So many people on this Earth walk around feeling a lack of self worth. Their ego controls their existence. It's so important to recognize that we are Divine beings. This is our truth. As we step into this awareness, we step into our wholeness. We all have *stuff* that happens to us along our life's journey. Once we get past the initial pain of it, we have a choice. We can allow it to contribute to a sense of *inferiority*, or we can take these experiences and have them serve in the development of our wisdom. The very fact that we were born makes us worthy. Life happens. We all mess up and we all experience pain. It's part of our *humanness*. The truth is, we're all figuring it out along the way, just like everyone else.

As *human beings*, we are a beautiful blend of primal physical existence and the Divine. Love is the essence of our true *beingness*. It is what connects our consciousness to one another and to Source. The fact that we can feel love and give love means that we are an extension of Source energy- the Divine. Anything else is an illusion. As we come to understand this, we also get to experience bliss in all aspects of life.

"Every man knows that his highest purpose in life cannot be reduced to any particular relationship. If a man prioritizes his relationship over his highest purpose, he weakens himself, disserves the universe, and cheats his woman of an authentic man who can offer her full, undivided presence."

- David Dieda, "The Way of the Superior Man"

Purpose

"The purpose in life is a life full of purpose."
- Robert Byrne; American, World Class Chess Champion

Placing your purpose in life before your relationship is one of the greatest gifts you can give to your relationship. A man with a purpose is a man with a presence and a man with a presence is the biggest turn on that a woman will find. A man with presence doesn't even have to speak to make our knees go weak; it's his authenticity, the way he carries himself, his body language, the way he looks into our eyes and sees inside of our soul, and the way he breathes us in. No woman can resist such a man.

Never sacrifice your vision or your purpose for your woman and your family. You will appear weak and spineless. It will contaminate the passion in your relationship and the romance will fizzle out. Weak behavior in a man may even disgust a woman as it does not create a sense of safety. She will not feel free to let go, and may end up trying to be in control all the time. She may even test you on this, because that is also a trait of the feminine nature. We don't test you to be mean, but because at the core of our essence we need to know that you are our warrior, and a warrior stands up for what he believes in. A warrior does not crumble.

It is important to a man to feel needed. You are much happier in a relationship when you feel like the hero. This is part of your masculine nature. It comes from living your life with purpose. When a woman understands this, she can give you the space to be just that. What women long for is to feel cherished. When your woman receives this gift from you, you become her hero. She will feel more inspired to reinforce her appreciation for the role you play as the hero in her life through her words and actions.

When one partner takes on the role of the parent, it can be poison to the relationship. Do not do it to her and do not allow her to do it to you. In many relationships a woman takes on an unhealthy pattern of mothering their man which leads to nagging. It may be she feels he is weak, or she learned it by witnessing her mother do it to her father. Allowing this is as harmful as doing it.

Taking on sibling roles with one another is a direction you want to avoid as well. For example, purposely belching and passing gas around one another does not contribute to romance. Taunting and feeling competitive as you would around your brother or sister may have a playful element, but it does not contribute to romance. There are much better ways to be playful in your relationship. If you want to keep romance sizzling, save that kind of buddy play for your pals outside of your relationship. Remember in addition to being friends, you are also lovers. For a woman to be aroused sexually, she has to first be aroused on a romantic level emotionally. Making her laugh is a great start, then the more a woman senses your presence, safety, your love, and how you cherish her, and the beauty you see in her, the more turned on she will be.

I was once in a relationship with a man who had great difficulty making decisions. It drove me crazy. I felt I always had to be in control. Even when we made plans to go to a restaurant, I would ask him where he wanted to go and he would say, "Where ever you want, dear." His intentions were good. He was trying to please me, but it drove me nuts. I just wanted him to stand his ground, be in his presence, and make a decision even if I wouldn't have liked his choice. I would hear myself nagging him and complaining to the point where I hated the sound of my own voice. I would intentionally test and taunt him, just to see some fire come from him. I wanted to feel him assert himself and stand up to me, just so I knew he had it in him.

I suspect this weakness was a side effect of his having been raised by an unhealthy and verbally abusive father. His most important male role model never taught him self-confidence or how to be present. His relationships with women suffered because of it. After I walked away, I watched as he continued to struggle in his relationships because he did not know how to be present in his warrior essence. If you were a victim of an abusive father and recognize yourself in this scenario, do what you need to do to rise above the effects. Chances are, your father's father was abusive as well. Seek therapy, do inner work or anything else it takes to overcome the abuse.

I am not a therapist, but I do use my own experiential process which has had much success in helping men release unhealthy father issues. I take them in their minds to a place and time where they see their parent's parent inflicting the same abuse upon them. Once my client is able to see his parent as the permanently wounded child who then grew up to inflict pain on their child, he is then able to alter his perspective. As the image of the abusive, overbearing father or mother shifts to that of a weak and confused child, the energy of resentment and pain can then be transformed to compassion and forgiveness.

If you were an abused son and are still suffering from the pain, I suggest reevaluating your need for your parent's approval. Understand that your abusive mother or father did not even approve of himself or herself. A person cannot give what they don't already have. When a person loves who they are, they treat others with love. When they feel pain and are not evolved, they tend to inflict pain. It is always sad when a child does not receive the guidance and love they deserve. If you are reading this book, then there is a good chance you are blessed with a woman who loves you and sees the love in you. Use this love as your strength. You have an incredible opportunity to break the pattern of the generations before you. Acknowledge your magnificence as the loving and Divine being that you are, and free yourself to be the man with a purpose that you were born to be.

"To love someone is to acknowledge the goodness of who they are. Through loving a person we awaken their awareness of their own innate goodness. It is as though they cannot know how worthy they are until they look into the mirror of our love and see themselves."

- JOHN GRAY, AUTHOR

"Your Path of Least Resistance leads to all the good that you desire. So as you make a determination that you're going to be a big time savorer; a big time complimenter, and a hardly ever criticizer; a big time appreciator and a hardly ever noticer of something wrong; and a big time lover, and a hardly ever hater; and a big time reacher for thoughts that feel good--as you are reaching for these thoughts that feel best, you are automatically finding your Path of Least Resistance. And when you find your Path of Least Resistance, you are connected to your source of clarity and abundance and physical stamina, and Well-being."

- ABRAHAM-HICKS

The First Step

Finding *clarity* is the first step toward making your dream business a reality. In order to receive what we want, we need to be very clear about what it is that we want. It sounds simple enough, but when we are too close to our own thoughts, sometimes we have to dig a little to find the clarity we need to move forward.

Clarity is important for your vision and how you market your business. The more vague the marketing, the fewer clients you'll attract. The more vague the vision, the longer it will take to materialize. How clear are you on your vision? What intention have you and your partner set for yourselves?

Discuss this with your beloved. Make sure you and she have the same intention for your business. Create a vision board together and keep it in a prominent place in your office where you can see it every day. Plan to spend a whole evening creating your vision board, and make it a celebration. Lay out some special decadent treats, break out your favorite special beverage, and play some uplifting music. Be prepared with a variety of magazines, two pairs of scissors, paste, and a poster board to paste your vision onto. You can also write some inspirational words on your board to go along with your vision. You may even want to cut the board in half and create your own separately. Then, when you are complete, put them side by side and see how they flow together. Having this visual of your dream as a constant reminder is a great tool for clarity.

Picture your vision in your mind's eye as though it already exists, and feel the beautiful emotions which come with that. Make it a game as you create your own virtual reality in your imagination. You only have to do this for a few minutes each day. Combining the clarity of your vision and your ability to feel joy as if you are already living it will transform the vision into reality with greater ease. Stay in a place of wonderment as you imagine how it may materialize without being attached to the "how." Then, take inspired action toward it and miracles can happen. I have created a meditation CD designed to help with this process titled "*Opening to Abundance.*" You can purchase this CD on my website under the "*Products*" link.

Once you are both clear on your vision, your next step is to be clear on your objective. Why do you want what you want? What do you hope to achieve? How will it serve others? What purpose does it have? Why do you believe you can achieve it? Write down these questions and give a copy to your partner. Answer them individually and then compare notes and see how your answers weave together. In my experience, many people get stuck on the belief part. They have trouble believing that all those wonderful things they desire can really happen to them. If you experience this doubt in yourself, just remember it's only your ego trying to keep you safe and within your comfort zone. You're a Divine loving, creative being, remember? This simple fact makes it possible for anything you desire to come into your life, particularly when your desire is the highest good for yourself and others.

Now you will need to define your sense of direction. It took me a while to get this one. For the longest time, I aimed to help everyone but too few were interested. When people looked at my website, they couldn't figure out who I was talking to. Once I made the decision to work specifically with entrepreneurial couples, my business became well defined. This strengthened my sense of direction and ability to focus. I was still doing the same work, only now I'm more specific on who I am speaking to, and my marketing became very clear and precise.

Choosing a niche can be especially challenging and troublesome for women due to our nurturing nature. We want to take care of everyone and fear that by choosing one specific group, we are leaving people behind. I used to say to myself, "but what about those people over there? I can take care of them too. I like working with them too." Once I realized my niche was not a life long commitment, and that I could expand and broaden my niche through time, it became a much easier decision. I love working with couples. Then, after a year of serving my fabulous clients through The Playful Partership, I chose to expand and create SensualSage.com, dedicated to just women. I have the freedom to make that choice. My heart's desire of working more closely with women and helping them align with their Feminine life force is being fulfilled. They are my primary focus now. For the women with whom I create a close client/coach relationship with, they don't have to go to someone else in the event they want to receive coaching with their beloved. The Playful Partnership is there for them.

As a woman realizes she has the freedom to expand her choices as her business grows, choosing a niche becomes a much easier task.

So, what if your woman is having problems choosing a target market? First of all, stop using the words *target market.* They just do not resonate with women. It sounds like we're aiming to shoot at something. *Niche* is a word which resonates more with the feminine psyche. I personally like the word *tribe* best. Next, try to get her on the same page with you as you explain how she can expand her choices, or change her mind completely down the road as the business grows. She just has to decide who her tribe is now. You have to know who you are talking to, or they will not hear you, and you will attract no one, or at least very few. The more specific your tribe, the more you will be recognized as a specialist. As a specialist, you can charge much higher fees.

You want to have layers to your business, commonly referred to as the *funnel.* I actually prefer the pyramid model. This is where you offer a high end service right at the top. It's a much faster way of building momentum in your business, and easy to do when you are a specialist in your field. Whether you use the funnel model or the pyramid, you have the products, services and information you offer at the outset, then take your clients deeper. Then, you can think about broadening and expanding it.

Men, in contrast to women, have no issues picking a *target market.* That's because of your single-minded focus. This explains why many women have trouble learning from male marketing coaches. They tell us to just pick a target market and go for it. That works great for you, but not for us. We need more guidance on seeing clearly which niche we can serve best and how.

It's a good idea to reevaluate your direction every year anyway. Marketing trends are changing all the time. Once she understands that it's all about finding her tribe, and that it does not have to be a permanent decision, it will help your beloved relax and work with you to choose one direction, right now and go for it. You also have to make sure you both love the people you choose to work with. It's a lot more fun and provides us with greater incentive when we love our clients. We always have a choice. Choosing the path which feels more playful is a guarantee that you are going in the right direction.

I am a Certified Niche Breakthrough Secrets coach. I will quickly resolve any niche turmoil you or your beloved may have by guiding you through the Niche Breakthrough Secrets process. In just one day you will both know exactly what your ideal tribe is, so you can eliminate any indecisiveness that may be holding you back from moving your business forward.

Ok, so now you have set your intention. You have a vision and the direction is becoming clearer. Do you have a plan? Start with a 90 day plan of action that incorporates a firm goal. Once you have accomplished that, set another. Sit down with your partner and work out clearly where you want to be one year, three years and five years from now. Write all of this down on paper, so you have a visual. What does your life look like as you look ahead? What is your first plan of action to get there? What resources will you need? What kind of a feedback system do you have outside of your relationship? Remember, you can be too close to see your own issues sometimes. Having others outside of your relationship to turn to for solid, honest feedback is a great asset to your business.

These are all very important questions to be sorting through together to achieve clarity. This clarity will be valuable in maintaining harmony in your relationship, by preventing conflicts brought on by assumptions or lack of preparation. Remember, it all starts with a clear understanding of your true intention clearly communicated with your partner. Once you have that in place, taking the next step, then the next, becomes a much simpler journey.

I have aided thousands of participants in finding clarity in their intentions. One of the things I often see them get tripped up with is confusing the intention with the *how*. For example, I once had a participant in a workshop whose intention was to manifest two million dollars. She was having such great difficulty with the process she was at the point of tears. I asked her, "Why do you want two million dollars?" She replied, "So I can open my own school and spend more time with my daughter." I said, "Well, that's your intention, not the money." The money was the *how* she felt she needed to make her intention happen. The *how* is not our job. The Universe will take care of that. She may acquire a business partner, find an investor, or benefit from any number of possibilities that will bring about school and more free time with her daughter. When we get attached to how we think it has to happen, and focus on that one thing, we are limiting our possibilities. As I explained this to the woman, her entire body relaxed and she moved through the process with ease. It was a huge ah-hah moment for her. Be absolutely clear on what it is you both really want and give that your attention. Let go of any thoughts of *how* you believe it's going to show up, and instead shift to a place of wonderment and anticipation of its arrival.

When people focus on how much money they feel they need to achieve their intentions, it can be stressful and actually slow down the flow of the money. When this happens, what is being focused on is the lack of something, so lack is what will continue to show up. When we go to that place of wonderment and anticipation instead, we open up the flow. When we hold onto the belief and knowledge that what we want will show up, it will. We just have to keep our eyes on the prize and continue to take inspired action toward it.

The quote by Abraham-Hicks says it all. The best way to find clarity is to follow the path of least resistance, no matter what your rational mind may be saying at the time. The voice to listen to is what you are feeling in your heart and solar plexus, not the chatter in your head. Your head contains knowledge, but your heart is your source of wisdom, and the solar plexus is where we hold our emotions. Our emotional guidance system is the GPS to our inner truth and clarity

If the thought of going in one direction ties your stomach up in knots, chances are you are looking down a road which will not lead to your ultimate happiness and success. Do not confuse this with the fear that comes from breaking out of your comfort zone as you move to the next level of success. That kind of fear is usually accompanied by a layer of excitement. I'm talking about that knot you get in your gut as an initial reaction. It's like the one you may have felt when you met a person who you were considering as a potential client, only to find later that working with that person was, or would have been, a big mistake. That knot was your inner wisdom telling you to beware. It is something you always want to pay attention to. If you feel a sense of ease or excitement when making a decision, it's your emotional guidance system providing clarity, saying, "Yes, go this way!" When you act on this feeling, you are taking inspired action.

Miracles happen every day. People and things come into your life in the most unexpected ways. The words of Martin Luther King say it all, "You don't have to see the whole staircase, you just have to take the next step." That first step does require a leap of faith, but it is an important piece of the formula to make your dreams come true.

Whatever we focus on will expand every time- no exceptions. Sometimes it's wise to get a little bit of guidance to help us stay on track and keep focusing on the things which make our heart sing, and release what no longer serves us.

When you go to visit ThePlayfulPartnership.com, you'll see an opt in box, at the upper right hand corner where you can sign up to receive my training videos, audios, articles, words of wisdom, and inspiration emailed directly to your inbox. It's a good place for you and your beloved to receive that guidance you may be looking for to create and maintain harmony in business, and throw some fuel onto the fire and passion you have for one another for a more blissful sex life.

PART TWO:

THE PHYSICAL REALITY

"Work, love and play are the great balance wheels of man's being."

- Orison Swett Marden, author (1850 - 1924)

Creating Space

Setting the stage properly for your work environment will make a huge difference in the flow of your business. How you set up your space will vary depending on whether you are running your business in or away from your home. If your business is not at home, then you have an easy advantage in keeping your work space separate from your living space.

Be conscious of how you feel as you go about your work day. Do you find yourself feeling distracted or unmotivated? If so, it could be the result of a cluttered work space. Keeping your space tidy and clear of clutter will help to keep your thoughts free of clutter and distractions. A little bit of organized chaos is okay. Just be aware. You can feel when the clutter is interfering with your flow. Everything in existence is made up of energy. If your space is cluttered, that clutter is contributing to blocking the energy of your space, which in turn blocks productivity. There is a reason Fung Shui is such a popular and thriving business- it works. Fung Shui is the art of placement through the awareness of energy, creating balance and harmony in your living and working environment. When your space is balanced it enhances balance within you. This induces greater productivity.

You may feel that your space is not quite set up as you'd like, but you're not sure what to do about it. I recommend hiring a Fung Shui specialist. You may only need a few pointers on how to rearrange your environment to create a more productive space. In the meantime try rearranging your furniture. You may be surprised at the difference this will make, especially if your working life feels stagnant right now. It could be as simple as your space having been stale and unchanging for too long. By creating a shift in your office's physical space, you can also create a shift in your productivity.

If you or your partner feel overwhelmed by chronic clutter habits and are unsure how to begin tackling them, then the habit is most likely a symptom of something much deeper. In this case, a good professional organizer can help you find the source of the habit so you will not only free your space of clutter, but prevent it from reoccurring.

If your work space is in your home, it is imperative that you create a complete separation between the space you work in and the space you live in. If you already have a home office with its own room and a door that closes after work hours, great! Hopefully this office is at the opposite end of your home from your bedroom. Placing an office in the middle of the home places business energy at the center of the home environment and everything revolves around it. This is not good. If this is the case with you, I suggest you switch your office with another room. Having your desk situated so you can look out a window while you work will give you a greater sense of space. If that's not possible, place it so it's facing into the room. Avoid a desk facing close to a wall. The energy has no where to flow and becomes blocked. A renovated garage dedicated to your business can make an ideal home office space. Not only do you have a separate room for your business, but it's detached from your house. That's a good thing. You can always purchase a little supply shed for your tools and garden supplies.

If budget is an issue and you do not have a separate room for your office, then get creative. Having your desk and work area in a space visible from any part of your living space is detrimental to your sexual health. Imagine, there you are curled up with your beloved on the sofa watching a movie, or listening to some stimulating music, and the sexual energy starts to stir. You can feel the heat building in your body and your woman's. Suddenly, her multitasking gets activated as she looks over and sees the pile of work on the desk and says, "Don't let me forget to do a follow up with that new client on Monday." Bam! She's back at the office making decisions. Her masculine essence has surfaced and the polarity of your sexual essence is now out of balance. Your love making skills may be able to bring her back, but the fact is, the office is still there in plain view. Being the woman that she is, if she sees it, she'll be thinking about it. Get the damn office out of sight! Sorry, didn't mean to yell… yes I did. I cannot stress enough how important this is. This alone can throw a huge wrench into the flow of your romance.

So, what to do with no separate room available for an office? I had an apartment that drove me crazy when I first moved in because there was no foyer. You walked in the door and you were suddenly in my living room. I hooked up a curtain rod onto my ceiling in the shape of an arc right at the entrance. I then hung a ceiling-to-floor length curtain which was able to open and close easily along the tracking rod. It worked like a charm. It created a foyer with flexibility and it looked great. You can buy this tracking rod at any Home Depot store. It's the same rod designed to hang a curtain in the window. The rings to hang up the curtain go inside the tracking. The rod is flat and bends easily to any shape you want. You can secure it with anchors into the ceiling. When office hours are closed, you can slide the curtain shut, hiding any sign of your business. Folding room partitions are also a great solution. They are easy to find and very affordable. They can enhance the décor of the space and make a huge difference in separating your work from your play. I personally love the curtain. With the ceiling-to-floor cover, it completely conceals your office after hours.

If your office is at a window, then you may not like having a partition or curtain, because you won't want to block the window. Even if you end up just throwing a large piece of fabric over your work area to get it out of site for the time being, do it. Get creative and do what it takes to make it happen-out of sight, out of mind. Your minds have much more enjoyable places to wander to on your time off than places that remind you of work.

If tearing yourself away from your computer at night is an issue for you, then take steps to insure your time is balanced out. A great way to do this is to set your alarm clock for a shut down time. When that alarm goes off, close the office door and leave the lap top and all your work papers behind. If you don't have a door to close, then tuck them out of sight. You may feel some withdrawal symptoms at first, but this additional time will create the balance you need to enjoy an intimate relationship with your partner. You may be tempted to tell yourself that you just need to get one more job out of the way, then you can make time for your private life. The fact is, when you are self employed, there is always one more task to be done. It is never complete.

If you keep telling yourself that there is no time for play, then no play will show up in your life. If you decide play is important and you make space for pleasure, then pleasure is what you will experience. Of course, there will be exceptions when there are strict deadlines to meet. However, if the jobs with deadlines keep on coming and your life revolves around them, it's up to you to break the pattern. Trust me, life is much more fun with playtime. The things you desire flow into your life with much greater ease when you are aligned with what feels good, and playtime is guaranteed to make you feel good. You'll be rejuvenated and able to show up at the job with greater clarity. With your face turned constantly toward the grindstone, your vision is prevented from seeing and receiving opportunities.

Because of your driving force, hunt and kill instinct, single focus and the adrenaline rush this all creates, you have the ability to keep working for weeks on end and then take your time off once the task is done. Women cannot work this way. It works for the masculine, but it leaves us exhausted and drained. Remember, women are natural nurturers. That is our strength. So to maintain our strength it is imperative that we take time out on a regular basis to be nurtured. It is food for us. We need this consistent nourishment in our daily lives. We need at least one full day off a week to nurture and fill ourselves back up.

If you want to keep the passion in your playtime, you've got to make space in your day to savor one another, and create a sacred space for it to happen. This is imperative. It's natural when starting a business that there will be added enthusiasm for it. This enthusiasm may even trigger some sexual excitement. If you don't let go of the business talk at some point, it will have the reverse effect and the business will dominate your life. Maybe you're already there and that is why you purchased this book. I've certainly been guilty of over-working, pushing too hard, thinking, "I just need to get this project out of the way, then I'll take time for me." The truth is, once that project is done, there will be another, then another.

The only way we can enjoy a personal life and savor our loved ones is to make it a priority. When we don't, we get burned out, it affects our mood as well as our energy levels. This doesn't serve our business, our relationships, or our health. Energy is everything and whatever we give our focus to expands. When we don't give enough focus to savoring those we love, that part of our life will contract and diminish. Make space in your day, every day, to look into one another's eyes, to get out of your heads, and connect to your love. When you make space to make love, you are creating and maintaining a powerful energy in your lives which, in addition to making your life a beautiful experience, can generate fuel to supercharge your business. I'll get into more detail later on how you can actually channel your sexual energy to create prosperity in all areas of your life.

"The most effective form of birth control I know is spending the day with my kids."

- Jill Bensley

The Little People

If you also share your home or office space with children, then you really have your hands full. Make sure your living space is arranged so you can enjoy the treasured moments you call your own when the kids are in bed without the clutter of children's toys. Sponge Bob and baby dolls are not exactly conducive to romance, although you could make good use of lego toys by building a wall to keep the rest of the toys out of sight. Toss a sensuous piece of fabric over the children's area, throw in some soft lighting and the entire room can shift from a vibe of kiddy playtime to passionate play in a matter of minutes. Game of doctor anyone?

If you are a parent with a home office and preschool children, but feel your budget does not allow for a nanny, you may want to shift your perspective. Ask yourself how much more work you could get done if you had help? How would that translate into additional income? Could you use that additional income to pay for child care? It would free you up to focus more freely on your work during business hours, making it possible to grow the business more quickly.

In the meantime, let's say you don't have a nanny and are working on the business with children to look after. Not only is this distracting, but quite a juggling act. I bow down to you for even attempting it. Perhaps I can offer a suggestion which may help make things a little easier. Your work can seem very strange to your children compared to the toys and games they have to play with. You don't want to fall into the trap of using the TV as a baby sitter. There are few shows that really contribute to the growth of your child. A great way to help keep your child occupied and make them feel involved in your business is to create their own little private office space. You can purchase a child's musical and educational laptop for less than $40. It will stimulate them and help keep them busy while you do your work. Give them their own little chair at their own little desk with papers to shuffle and their own cup with pens and pencils, their own make believe phone, files, post it notes and anything else you can think of. Now they have their own little office just like mommy and daddy. As you run your business, they will feel more connected to yours.

If you know your inability to savor the romance you desire is due largely to your role as a parent, it's time to make some adjustments. I'm sure you choose to put your children first, and understandably so. Remember, however, that we teach by example more than by what we say. If your love life is not a priority in your family, think about the message your children will pick up and what they will expect for their own families. Patterns repeat themselves. You will be teaching them that taking time to share love with one another is not important, that it's all about work and taking care of everyone but yourselves. Is this the model you want them to follow? Children love to witness their parents expressing their love for one another. It sets a great example and provides an added sense of safety for them. You must make time to make love for the sake of your relationship and to assure the health of your children's future relationships. When intimacy is alive and well, it carries an energy outside of the bedroom which radiates throughout your household, and has a positive effect on everyone.

"Sex makes babies. So it is ironic that the child, the embodiment of the couple's love, so often threatens the very romance that brought that child into being. Sex, which set the entire enterprise in motion, is often abandoned once children enter the picture. Even when children come by a different route, their impact on the sex life of the couple is no less dramatic."

- Esther Perel, "Mating in Captivity"

It's quite common for a man to feel the lover in his woman slip away once a child comes into the equation. To say it's due to sleep depravation is to state the obvious, but it goes deeper than that. Most women love their sex to be sensual. Eroticism is not just a genital experience for the feminine. The caresses, the gentle touches, the scents, the sounds, all play a huge role in erotic stimulation for us. We also love a bit of animal ravenous sex as well, but the sensuality is especially important.

"In the physicality between mother and child lie a multitude of sensuous experiences. When they devour us with those big eyes, we are besotted, and so are they. This blissful fusion bears a striking resemblance to the physical connection between lovers."

- Esther Perel, "Mating in Captivity"

The skin of a baby is so soft and beautiful to touch, their smell is incredible and so is the way they move. Their little toes and fingers, and their beautiful eyes. They are captivating. A woman can get caught up in the sensual experience of caressing and breathing in everything about her new child until it fulfills her to the point she doesn't feel the need to reach for a sensual experience with her man. This is why it is so important to make extra effort to make sure time savoring one another actually takes place. The longer you refrain from making it a priority, the more disconnected you will feel as your sex life becomes a distant memory.

"Family life flourishes in an atmosphere of comfort and consistency. Yet eroticism resides in unpredictability, spontaneity, risk."

- Esther Perel, "Mating in Captivity"

Spontaneous, passionate play at home is wonderful, but if it doesn't seem to be happening for you, plan a date night. Hire a baby sitter or have a family member come and stay the night. Rent a hotel room and treat yourselves to a special evening with no distractions; just you and your Goddess and whatever unfolds. If you're concerned about the expense of date nights, then you need to ask how much they are worth to you. I believe they're a valuable investment. They will charge you with energy, which will create more productivity when at work. Sex is our life force. It is the most powerful energy we possess, powerful enough to create a new life. I don't need to tell you how much more playful life is when sex is an active part of it.

There are plenty of quaint bed and breakfasts in quiet and serene settings outside the city that rent for a very reasonable fee. Or go to a camp ground and pitch a tent. Fresh air can be very invigorating. Where there's a desire, there's a way to make it happen. Include it in your schedule and fulfill this commitment to one another. If you have to hire someone to watch the kids for a day, or take them for a sleep over at someone else's house, do it! Consider it a business investment. It will deeply enhance your relationship; it will energize you so you can concentrate more fully on your business. And, don't you dare turn this time into a business meeting. No shop talk allowed! It's a passion date, a time to savor your love and get steamy together. Have fun, go play and make love!

"I have to exercise in the morning before my brain figures out what I am doing."

- Marsha Doble

Become *the* Body

Exercise

If you are not already in an exercise program, then get with the program! Our bodies are designed to move. Start your day with a run, yoga, time at the gym, a jump for joy… anything. This will work miracles for your professional and personal lives. It gives you energy, it makes your mind sharp, it releases endorphins, and it is great for the sex drive. Both you and your partner will experience a huge shift in your well being, harmony at work, and your playtime at home. If you've been thinking about it but just haven't gotten around to it, it's time to make it happen. Get off your butt and take action. It will create magic in your life. It will prevent many issues from developing in the first place, simply because of how great you'll both feel about yourselves and your bodies. My advice is to find something that's fun for you. Exercise can even be playful. The more fun you have, the more you'll want to do it. Dance is my favorite form of movement. Maybe you enjoy kicking or hitting a ball. Whatever it is, just get up, get out, and play.

The Energy of Food

For this section I would like to acknowledge one of my mentors, Jeffrey Armstrong, who is a world expert on Vedic teachings and who taught me much of what I share here

The Vedic teachings contain three concepts known as the Gunas, or Processes of Matter. They include Sattva, Rajas, and Tamas. These three stages are also the three energy forms that relate to our food. Sattva means "service" for the good of all. This is the energy of enlightenment. It is happiness and nurturing. Sattva is our connection to the Divine, harmony, and peacefulness. Food in this category includes live food necessary for our maintenance, such as fresh vegetables, fruit, and legumes. Plant-based food has the most life when it is raw or only lightly cooked. There is a good reason why raw food is becoming so popular now. Enriching our bodies with live food makes us feel healthier, lighter, and more energized to keep up with our busy lives. We are living beings, we need live enzymes to be healthy. When we eat live food, we take in more life and are therefore more likely to have a longer and better quality future.

Rajas is the energy of enlivenment. It is activity, creation, pain, agitation, desire, and selfishness. Examples of this in food are fish and meat. Animal-based food is energy, but we have to be careful about the quantity you put into your body. Studies have shown that consuming more that 20% of your diet in meat may increase your risk for cancer. Rajas is the mode of passion and intense focus. For example, athletes who exert their energy with focus and purpose to attain a result are Rajasic. When athletes push their energy to far, it results in pain and injury.

Tamas is the energy of endarkenment. It is destruction, uncaring, ignorance, inertia, misery, catabolism, and torment. A drunken man flailing about exerting physical energy without focus is Tamasic. Basically, in relation to food, it is anything which is dead. This is all processed food. A recent Harvard study found that moderate red meat and pork consumption doesn't actually increase heart-disease risk as previously thought, but processed red-meat and pork consumption drastically increases the risk of heart disease. Diet food is one of the worst offenders of processed food. Most diet food is packaged up processed junk which has no life in it. Often the marketing is based on the products being low in fat, but if you read the labels closely, you will find they are very high in refined, processed sugar. Shelves in the center aisles of grocery stores are full of dead food. That's why a nutritionist will tell you to only buy your food from the outer aisles, which will serve your body the best. The stuff in the middle aisles may seem alluring, but is probably because many of the unhealthy ingredients are addictive and will not serve you. It doesn't take a genius to figure out that Tamasic food- dead food- does not contribute to a healthy lifestyle. You are what you eat. If you eat dead food, you will not have a whole lot of energy in you. You may experience short-lived sugar highs, but in the long run, you will feel tired and depleted.

When we awake in the morning and first open our eyes, we are in a Tamasic state. We then start to move our body to get some energy going, that is Rajas. After some movement, we hopefully shift into Sattva.

The deity associated with Sattva is Vishnu. In Hindu teachings, Vishnu carries a wish for the good of all and oversees preservation and maintenance. The deity associated with Rajas is Brahma. The daily alteration of light to dark is attributed to the activity of Brahma. The deity associated with Tamas is Shiva. Shiva is the destroyer. He is associated with the darkness. Now, all three of these are necessary elements to our existence. When a tree dies in the forest, its trunk, leaves and branches rot. This is Tamas. When they go into and become part of the earth, they become Rajas, providing fertilizer and creating energy for the new plants to grow. Sattva is the energy of the plant itself, full of light and maintaining life. It's the cycle of all life.

What it all boils down to is this: what you eat, you become. If you know you are eating a lot of food which is Tamasic, then you are in fact contributing to the premature death of your body. If you are eating a diet high in Rajas, monitor your portions. You may be giving your body energy, but too much can lead to aggression and an overload of energy can lead to, as the research shows, cancer. Food which is Sattva always serves our bodies and we can never have too much of it. I'm not saying you should never eat cake again. There is a place for pleasure food, especially when we give ourselves permission to savor it as opposed to feeling guilt. Balance and common sense is the key here.

There was a period of about four years when I read diet and nutrition books cover to cover, like novels. Most of them were written by doctors, yet I found most contradicted one another. The one thing they did all agree on, however, was the importance of always eating lots of fresh fruit and vegetables. The vegetables highest in minerals are the dark green leafy ones. The fruit highest in fiber and vitamins are those darker in color, such as berries. The more fresh fruit and veggies you have in your diet, the more Sattva you will be, the more nurtured and peaceful your body and mind will feel, and the more harmony your body will have within. How you appear on the outside is always a reflection of what is happening on the inside. Ask yourself, what do I want to become? Then eat that.

What's Your Type?

Ayervedic teachings include a concept known as the Doshas. These are the body types. There are three primary body types known as Kapha, Pitta, and Vatta. Putting all possible combinations of these together, we end up with 10 different body types. This is a particularly fascinating subject. It is not just a theory. It is a fact that every human on the planet is one of these 10 body types. This knowledge has been part of the Ayervedic teachings for thousands of years. What's also fascinating is that each body type has specific character traits which come with it. This is something we are born with and will always be part of who we are. When it comes to relationships, some body types are more compatible together than others. This knowledge will give you great insight and understanding into your nature as well as that of others, including your partner.

We each have elements of all three body types. It is rare, but there are some who have a perfect balance of all three. For most, one is dominant with another as a strong secondary and traces of the third. The element of Kapha is water. Their bodies tend to be very curvatious, large or overweight. A common trait of a Kapha is that they can easily skip breakfast and go hours into the day before eating. They are also the body type most prone to weight gain. They can be drawn to indulge in empty carbs and when they skip meals, which can happen often, they end up binging late at night. Kaphas are also the nurturers. They tend to be calm and are the ones who like to take care of people. If a fight were to break out in a room, there's probably a good chance the person making sure everyone was ok has Kapha as their primary body type. Kaphas are the ones who hold it all together.

Vattas are the element of air and space. Their bodies are often slim and slender. They tend to be refined and move very gracefully. They are very sensitive to their surroundings. They tend to have a nervous energy. They can also be very analytical. If someone is having a difficult time trying to figure out which body type they are, they are probably a Vatta. It is common for Vatta to have cold hands and feet all the time. Their breakfast habits can vary. Sometimes they will go a long time without breakfast, sometimes they will eat first thing in the morning. If a fight were to break out in a room, the Vatta would be the one wanting to stay as uninvolved as possible.

Pittas do not like to skip breakfast. In fact, they need to eat as soon as they wake up. This is because their element is fire, so they burn off what they eat more quickly. They tend to be medium build with well defined muscles. They can also be very opinionated and direct. They make excellent athletes and strong speakers. If a fight were to break out in a room and the two involved were really engaged, there would be a good chance they'd both be primarily Pitta body types. I'm taking a guess that Tony Robbins is primarily a Pitta body type with Kapha as his secondary type. He has a strong muscular body, a firey outgoing personality and is a very successful speaker. In his past, before his speaking years, he had trouble with weight gain, which would be the Kapha influence. He also has a desire to care for others, which is also a Kapha quality.

Oprah is likely Kapha/Pitta. She has the round curvy body shape and has had to work to maintain her weight. She is also wonderful at caring for others. With Pitta being her secondary type, she is strong in her opinions and not shy about communicating them openly and publically.

The best body type for a fashion supermodel to have would be a Vatta with Pitta as the secondary type. With the Vatta body being naturally slender, maintaining a model's body could be done in a healthy manner. With Pitta as the secondary type, a model would have the fire and aggression needed to endure and stand out in the modeling industry. I personally look forward to the day when high fashion represents all body types. However, until then the Vatta/Pitta combination would adjust more naturally to this career choice.

Are you beginning to recognize yourself from these descriptions? If you're still confused and can't figure out which one you are, no worries. You're probably a Vatta.

It's best to pair up with someone of a different body type in order to complement each other. For example, if two Kaphas are together, they run the risk of becoming a couple of couch potatoes. Pitta and Kapha go well together. With water as Kapha's element, they can handle Pitta's fire and know how to cool them down when they get a bit over heated. Pitta's fire is good for them because it helps keep the Kapha moving preventing them from becoming lazy.

A Vatta woman would be very attracted to a Pitta man. She would be drawn to his heat, and the sense that he'll protect her. The Pitta would be attracted to her refinement. However, over time, the Pitta would begin to wear her down. She is too sensitive for him. With air and space as her element, the fire would expand too much for her. In the case of a not so conscious Pitta man, he could even become abusive. Vatta and Pitta are not a good combination for an intimate relationship. If you and your partner recognize yourselves in this scenario, you can, now that you have more awareness about it, work through it from a new perspective. It may take some effort, however where there is love and conscious awareness, a great shift can take place.

What if you suspect you and your partner are of the same body type? This knowledge will help make you aware of your need to work together to turn your potential weaknesses into strengths.

This is a very involved topic and I've only given you a tiny taste of it. In my coaching programs, I touch a bit more on this and help clients figure out what their body types are. Once you have this clarity, instead of pushing against the inevitable, you can embrace the differences in one another, understand how to better complement one another, and use the differences to your advantage.

Supplements

It's always a good idea to supplement a healthy diet with a multivitamin. Getting lots of vitamin C will help boost your immune system and a good B vitamin will help with stress. The vitamin B12 becomes more difficult to assimilate with age. You need to find a B12 vitamin which is a sublingual, meaning it dissolves under your tongue. Sublingual B12's go directly into the blood stream. Studies have shown that when we take a B12 in a form that is swallowed, our bodies only absorb about 2% of it. I used to sell a B12 supplement for a network marketing company, and many clients who purchased our sublingual B12 vitamin actually found they no longer needed antidepressant medication. A B12 deficiency can result in depression, low energy, and a variety of other symptoms. Getting a good B12 vitamin will boost your energy levels, help you deal with stress more effectively, and improve your overall sense of well-being.

Water

Unless you live in an unusual remote area, your tap water is toxic. The chemicals they have to add to source water to clean it of deadly bacteria are not intended for human consumption. The majority of bottled water is tap water with the same impurities but with the life stripped out of it, and it has an acidic pH. The Japanese, who are water experts, refer to it as "dead water." Over 90% of North Americans suffer from acidosis. An acidic pH creates an environment where disease and illness thrives. In an alkaline based environment, disease cannot exist. When our body is toxic, the brain is also affected and can contribute to toxic thoughts, resulting in negative mood swings. Through my own personal experience, I can testify that by drinking ionized alkaline water you can experience a calmer sense of inner being and increased energy. These are both beneficial to a productive business and a harmonious relationship.

As Source energy beings, we are capable of transforming our body to a state of wellness simply by being aware of our vibration. All disease is the result of dis-ease. Louise Hay is famous for bringing this knowledge out to the world in her book, "Heal Your Body." Mr. Masaru Emoto is known for his work on photographing water crystals as displayed in his book, "The Hidden Messages in Water." He attached paper with high vibration words such as "love," "angel," or "thank you" to containers of water and then photographed the water crystals. They appeared as beautiful crystal formations, like perfect snowflakes. When he took this same water and attached words of a low vibration, such as "you fool," or "you make me sick, I will kill you," the water crystals changed to dark ugly formations. This is remarkable scientific evidence of the effect our vibration has on our physical state. When you consider that our bodies are 70% water, it would be wise to be aware of the thoughts and feelings we project upon ourselves, and to do what ever it takes to send ourselves loving energy.

If you want to lose weight or gain muscle, try focusing on what you like rather than approaching it from an angle of what you dislike. Do you like your arms, your legs, your chest? Do you like the fact that you can walk, or run, or dance? Love the part of your body which is functioning the way you already want it to and start from there. We can achieve the transformation we desire much faster when we come from a place of self-loving instead of a place of self-loathing. When we start from a place of love, we are more mindful of what we put into our bodies and it becomes easier to eat what we wish to become.

Ionization produces a high alkaline, high vibration, anti-oxidant, and cellular absorption water. It is the healthiest available anywhere. If you use pH drops, at least your water is being alkalized, but it does not transform the water to cellular absorption or into an anti-oxidant. Cellular absorption hydrates six times more than regular water. Water which is a positive oxidation level contributes to the aging process. Anti-oxidant water reverses the aging process. My ionizers are the wisest purchases I ever made. I did my research, owned a couple of machines and now own what I feel are the superior products on the market. I love them so much, I have become a dealer. Both my machines have amazing features. If you'd like to find out more, go to my website and click on the "products" link. I have lots of information, including videos, so you can educate yourself more on how the ionization process works, and the amazing health benefits it provides. I'm very passionate about this subject. Why not give 70% of your body the best it can get?

Acidosis and dehydration in the body is the source of so much pain and disease. When the pH of the body shifts by drinking consistent amounts of high alkaline antioxidant cellular absorption water, miracles occur. When we transform the body's pH to alkaline and healthy hydration levels, we create an environment where disease cannot expand. Disease needs an acidic environment to thrive.

Go to ThePlayfulPartnership.com and visit the Products page to watch the demonstration videos and see for yourself. It is one of the best decisions you can ever make for you and your family. You will also find out how you can acquire a machine for yourself, even if you are on a tight budget. Never compromise on health. The vitality it will bring to your life, to your relationship, and your to ability to do business with greater clarity and focus is priceless.

Take Care

You are the only one in control of your body. We just get one to play with in this lifetime. It is a magnificent machine, with our cells rejuvenating and recreating themselves every moment of every day. Notice how, when you cut your finger, the body works so quickly to rebuild and repair the cells so you would never know you had an injury. The entire body, inside and out has the ability to transform in this way. It really is a miracle. If you don't like the condition of your body, then do something about it; transform it. Choose an exercise that feels like fun. Taking care of your body will help you show up in your business in a much more powerful way, and it will make it possible to have a long lasting healthy sex life. Reach your goals and be the lover of her dreams by becoming the body that will best serve you.

PART THREE:
GETTING THE JOB DONE

"Don't aim for success if you want it; just do what you love and believe in, and it will come naturally."

- David Frost

Focus

I touched on the subject of focus in the first section titled, *The Dance of the Masculine and Feminine.* This is a major subject regarding differences between men and women, how we do business and in the way it affects us on a personal level.

As a man, you especially understand the importance of focus and staying focused until the project is completed. Single focus is a beautiful gift that the masculine energy has to offer. I especially feel a deep respect for this masculine trait, probably because it's the one I've had to search for the deepest within myself. Women are wonderful at multitasking because the feminine is all about flow and movement. The problem this can create for woman with a strong feminine essence is that she may leave a trail of scattered, unfinished projects as she flows and moves from one thing to the next. It's been a life-long challenge for me to focus on one project and see it to completion without being distracted, and it's still is an ongoing task to maintain. I smile to myself as I work on focus to stay focused.

Put me on a dance floor and I can focus on dancing for hours. It's the ultimate expression of flow and movement for me. I also feel inspired through creativity. Since inspiration and creativity are aspects of feminine energy, the more inspired a woman feels, the easier it is for her to focus. If you have a creative personality then you know that the more inspiring a project is, the more focused you are to create. If your woman is having focus issues, help her find a way to creatively express herself and feel more inspired about the task at hand and I promise you will notice a difference.

I have talked about writing a book for years. I've talked about it for so long that I now have a collection of books inside me. I was finally able to focus on getting this one done because a woman named Donna Kozik developed a workshop called *Write a Book in a Weekend.* She facilitates the workshop by phone and internet, providing all the guidance and preparation we need to stay focused and feel supported throughout the journey. There were sixty of us busily writing away at the same time I began to write these words for you. All of us stayed focused on the task at hand because of the focused guidance of Donna and the inspiration she provided along the way. Granted, it took me a few months afterward to rewrite, edit, and add material. However, thanks to the guidance and inspiration she provided, I was able to decide what to write and act on it. In one weekend, I produced an incredible amount of information and my book was well under way.

Guidance, confidence, decision making, action, holding the vision; we need to tap into these masculine traits to get the job done regardless of our gender. Inspiration is focus fuel for women. Focus. It's what holds it all together and completes the job. As you both become aware of the role this masculine energy plays at work, you can better understand how it alters the polarity of your partner's masculine/feminine essence. With the scales tilted, sexual intimacy may not flow in the direction you would like. By understanding this, you can work together to help her shift back into her feminine, making it easier for intimacy to take place. I go into more detail on how to do this in Part Seven: *Making the Shift*.

The more masculine a man's essence, the more singular his focus. When a woman doesn't understand the singleness of her man's focus, it can cause unnecessary misunderstandings. I've seen it happen many times and I used to do it myself before I understood what was really going on. Women feel energy. We operate from our senses and emotions. The masculine is of the physical and mental. When you turn your focus from her onto something else, what she feels is your energy move away from her. She doesn't necessarily understand that you have to give this other thing all your focus and see it to completion before you can turn your focus back to her. This often trips women up. "But why is he over there, when I'm right here? Doesn't he love me? Doesn't he want to be with me? If he loves me, why does he want to be there?" Single focus. That's a gift you have.

So be patient with us. If your beloved business partner's attention has a tendency to wander from time to time, understand that the very thing that causes her to lose focus, is the same thing that makes you want to lay with her- her feminine essence.

A woman's ability to multitask can be of great value in business, provided it is coupled with structure. A woman moving about through her day in multitask mode may not understand just how irritating it can be for a man if she is constantly interrupting him. We can be in the middle of a job, talk on the phone, sort through files, surf the internet, do our nails and go over a "to do" list all at the same time. If you are experiencing issues with regard to your partner breaking your focus, help her understand it's a guy thing. Make eye contact with her so she feels your love, and gently explain that to finish the project at hand you need to be left alone to focus on one thing at a time. Once that's done, you can give her your undivided attention. An advantage of having your beloved as your business partner is that, once the office is closed, you can release the frustrations of this distraction with the attraction which caused it. Keep reading. Later in the book, I'll share some juicy tips on how to skillfully transform your professional adrenalin to playful bliss.

If your woman is having issues with focus and your business is suffering because of it, take a close look at the situation and see what you can do to help her stay on track. Inspiration is key here. Women can easily single focus when inspired by their work, and engaged in creative expression. In fact when they engaged in a task that is inspiring, they don't want their focus to be broken any more than you do. I am very inspired and creatively engaged as I write this book, I don't want to answer the phone, or anyone talking to me or interrupting my focus. It's been the ideal expression of single focus in my life.

Women love to be held accountable. Men would find it annoying to have someone checking in with them to see if they are staying on track. Not us. If it is done in a way that feels supportive, being held accountable works wonders for our productivity. The secret is to keep it fun. Life is not meant to be taken too seriously. Remember to celebrate your successes, no matter how small. The whole idea of work is to give us the freedom to play. Whenever you have the opportunity to make work feel like play, go for it.

My African dance teacher, Jacky Essombe, teaches choreography from the African village where she grew. One dance is based on the women walking out into the fields, breaking up the rocks and the soil, planting the crops, and harvesting them. Jacky explains that as the women labor in the fields. They sing and they dance together so it doesn't feel like work. They work together as a community to create an atmosphere of play and laughter. It's a celebration. We can learn a lot from these women. Find a way to make your work fun at every opportunity. There are many possibilities so there is no reason to dread going to work. If you really do not like the work you have chosen to do, then look for something which you can have more fun with. Life is too short. When we love what we do, staying focused requires much less effort.

If you and your partner are experiencing a lot of conflict in moving the business forward, you need to ask if this business you've chosen is really for you. Are you doing it because others have made money doing it, or because it excites you? Is it possible one of you is in the business only to support the other? This is admirable, but if it is causing conflict or unhappiness you need to reevaluate your direction. It's not fair to either of you. Whoever enjoys the business is not receiving all the support they could from the other, and the one who is not enjoying it is denying themselves something more fulfilling. If this resonates with either of you, you need to be honest with one another on this.

Notice the quote at the top of this section by David Frost - "Don't aim for success if you want it; just do what you love and believe in, and it will come naturally." As partners in love, running a business together needs to be fun or it will wear on your relationship and possibly destroy it. You can serve one another far better by helping the other find out what would turn them on, and supporting them on that path. Then, hire an assistant to help out with the business already in operation. You will need to make adjustments at first, but they could save your relationship and make life much more fun for both of you.

"If a woman suggests something that changes a man's perspective, then he should make a new decision based on his new perspective. But he should never betray his own deepest knowledge and intuition in order to please his woman or "go along" with her. Both she and he will be weakened by such an action. They will grow to resent each other, and the crust of accumulated inauthenticity will burden their love, as well as their capacity for free action."

- DAVID DIEDA

Role Playing

The role you each play in your business not only affects the dynamics of your professional relationship, it also has a direct effect on your personal relationship. Even if you are each in charge of a separate business, you are still in business together. You've got two businesses under the same roof and you are partners in love, functioning as one another's support system. This equates to being in business together. Yes, it's different from running the same business, but there is still a professional partnership at play. Regardless of which business makes more money, both businesses need to have equal priority. The support system must be as strong as the leadership. Feeling unsupported by your partner in any area of life creates a gap in the relationship. It also results in resentment and feeling underappreciated. The longer it continues, the more it will fester. So, no matter how busy either of you are, you need to make time in your day to listen to one another. Cheer each other on, with every success, no matter how small.

Offer honest feedback. Avoid telling your partner what would be a *better* way of doing things, or what they *should* do. This has the energy of judgment. Rather, use words such as, "this is what *works for me*, this is *what doesn't work*, and this is *what I would do differently*." Give one another permission to be completely honest and agree to receive their information, free of ego, observing and listening with detachment. Look at it as a simple puzzle to be solved. Clear solutions appear much more quickly this way and ideas flow more freely. A business is in a constant state of correcting and continuing, a series of little successes, all coming together to form one big success. As your business(es) thrive and move upward together, with each of you feeling fully supported by the other, abundance will be a natural byproduct. You will also find yourself having a greater appreciation for one another and the brilliance you each bring to the table.

Often when couples are running the same business, one partner is the dominant leader. Understanding each partner's strengths and weaknesses based on the dynamics of masculine and feminine energy will greatly serve you in this area. You already understand the necessity of utilizing masculine energy in the role of leadership. Regardless of who is playing this role, leadership is best played while consciously integrating feminine qualities. A good leader leads with compassion and intuition, two powerful feminine qualities. If you are the dominant leader in your business and you know intuition is not your strong suit, utilize this feminine gift by confiding in your woman often. When you are having difficulty with a decision, find out what her feelings are about the decision. Her intuition will be especially useful if you are considering doing business with someone you don't know. Any great business leader will tell you that intuition plays a strong role in the success of a business.

For years I worked in the film industry as an actress, stand in, photo double, and an extra. An extra is considered to be the bottom rung in the film business. I enjoyed it regardless, because I love being on set. I could always tell within a very short time after arriving what kind of leadership was running the show. If the director and/or assistant director was irritable and lacked compassion, their negative energy trickled all the way down to the bottom rung. You could feel the tension on those sets, as there was a lot of cranky energy going around. Making a film is a huge effort. There are numerous departments involved in getting the job done, the AD's, PA's, the grips, electrics, hair, wardrobe, catering, transport… hundreds of people on one set with a variety of jobs and personalities all working on the same project. When the disposition of the leader was infected by a bad attitude, it infected the entire show. When I walked onto a set with a fun loving director and AD who showed compassion, the difference was obvious. No matter how long the hours and how tired we became, the energy on set was delightful. We were happy to work a 15 hour shift when that was what it took to get the job done. Be a compassionate leader. When you verbally *acknowledge* and *appreciate* everyone you work with, no matter how menial their task, harmony will always result. Where there is harmony, there will be greater productivity, and greater results with your bottom line.

Obstacles in business are to be expected. How we move through them determines the quality of our character and the harmony of the work environment. If your partner is the primary leader, she has to tap into the masculine energy involved in decision making, focus, and control to run the show. When being in control reaches the point of being bossy and leaving the other feeling unappreciated or *less than,* problems will occur and egos will be triggered. Neither of you ever want to underestimate the value you each contribute. Expressing appreciation for the other's contribution needs to be a constant practice.

Being a couple in love and in the same business together puts you in a very unique situation. The fact is you are partners; you are a team. You are sharing your lives together and it so happens you are also in business together. I don't care who is at the helm, who is most in the public eye, who is playing the role of the leader, or who was the original creator of the business. You are a couple, which makes you partners. If the business was your creation before the two of you got involved, then I understand you have more of a vested interest in it. You feel like it belongs to you, like it's your baby. You may even feel like your partner is working for you. If your partner was the original creator of the business, then she probably feels the same way. The fact is, if one of you gets labeled as the boss and the other the employee, it will be a challenging dynamic to maintain, and, for the sake of your partnership, one I would advise against.

I recently met a man who runs his own consultation business. His wife is a bookkeeper. He expressed his frustration at the fact that she always puts her clients ahead of him and his bookkeeping is the last thing she takes care of. The business may be technically his, but as a couple, the success of the business has a direct effect on both of them. Maybe you recognize yourself in this scenario. If so, who ever is in the position of the bookkeeper needs to take care of their partner's books first. When you put the needs of clients before your own, it's a sign that there are boundary issues around money. It sends a message that clients are more important than you. When you put yourself and your partner first, you both feel nurtured and acknowledged, and therefore are able to be more fully present for your clients as well. The partner then feels supported and valued by the one they love. This prevents frustration from leaking into the personal relationship and fuels the business by saying, "you are important to me. I believe in you." This will help keep the business on track and moving forward. Keeping the books in order without delay also releases clutter which can otherwise block the flow of abundance in both business and intimacy.

It does not contribute to balance for the creator of the business to be taking a percentage of the net income while the other is on a fixed paycheck. If you developed the business on your own before the other came along, I understand why you would feel a greater attachment to it and the idea of splitting everything 50/50 may not feel comfortable. However, as partners, you must pay yourselves accordingly. If you're uncomfortable with this idea, then hiring an outside assistant may be a better option than using your partner in love as an employee. Maybe one of you has a more vested interest in the business, but what about the rest of your partnership? Often, when one partner puts in more hours with the business, the other puts in more time maintaining the home. So whether they assist you with the business, or put energy into the home, partners are partners. For both of you to feel valued equally, you must pay yourselves equally.

Ask yourself why anyone would go into business for themselves in the first place? The answer is usually along these lines: to have creative freedom and to be independent without having to take orders from anyone else. So, why would you want the boss/ employee dynamic woven into a love partnership? My coach, Kendall Summerhawk, is a great example, IAWBC is her coaching program. She is the face of the business. I became her client because of her brilliance and her energy. Behind the scenes her husband Richard Shapiro, runs the mastermind coaching calls, works one on one with clients, he even picks up the phone to call their clients just to say thank you and does who knows what else to make the business succeed. I guarantee Kendall does not see Richard as her employee. He is her partner in love and in business, never mind that she's the star of the show and the reason people sign up with her program. He's an expression of the Divine Masculine as he holds space for her and offers complete support. You can tell he loves his job and that Kendall acknowledges the role he plays as an integral part of the business. He is the leader in his area of the business, not a member of her staff.

If you have been functioning as the boss, it's time to adjust and think of your beloved as working *with* you, not *for* you. Ask yourself how important the work is that your partner does for you. Could you run the business without her? Is she happy in this role? If she's been the one playing the role of boss and it's causing discomfort or other issues for you, you need to sit down and calmly discuss a solution. Are you feeling a sense of purpose? Are you doing this work for the sole purpose of pleasing her? Is there something else you'd rather be doing? It's great to be supportive, but if it means sacrificing your sense of purpose, the stakes are too high. Having a sense of purpose is mandatory for a man. It is in your nature and without it you are incomplete. If this is the problem you are experiencing, the sooner you nip it in the bud and discuss it openly, the sooner you can bring it into balance. If you both decide to continue working together, then you need to shift your thinking and see yourselves as partners, communicate what that looks like, and come to an agreement. Committing it to paper can help with clarity, and clarity always contributes to the harmony of a relationship.

If you are the one at the helm, take a close look at what your partner does to help the business be successful. This is her specialty. Acknowledge it as such. This is the area of the business in which she is in charge. When you see this as her role, you can relax and do what you do best. You may have to delegate work to her which needs to get done. However, once you shift to acknowledging her as your support system, as opposed to an employee, you will feel a greater flow in your working relationship. She will feel more appreciated and acknowledged and therefore more inspired by the contribution she makes. When you redefine your business relationship in this way, a pleasant byproduct will be a more harmonious flow in your personal life.

If any of this is hitting a nerve with you, ask your partner to read this. Then, sit down, discuss it and express your feelings using the communication method I share in part 4, "The Art of Listening." A good leader knows how to follow and listen well. Never agree with her and just go along when in your heart you feel she is making a poor decision. It is imperative you speak your truth. Even if she doesn't like it at the moment, she will respect you for it. The role of leadership must be played with honesty, compassion and an open mind.

Feeling like an employee just doesn't work for your partnership in love. When you feel like your woman's hero, you are more fulfilled and have a greater sense of purpose. You feel more inspired to be of greater support to the business. It's important for each of you to be seen, heard, appreciated, and acknowledged in whatever role you are playing. When this happens, so does romance.

The more you work together, the clearer the individual gifts and contributions you each bring to the table will appear. What you want to avoid is an overlap of professional activities. Micro management will drive anyone crazy. Make yourselves crystal clear on who has what gifts and give that person their space to do their thing.

One of you may be more skilled at dealing with people on the phone than the other. Decide who does what and give one another the space to play the leadership role in that category. You are both working toward the same goal, but you cannot both do the same tasks, or you run the risk of butting heads as you each believe your way is better. This is a sure way of driving yourselves crazy and wanting to kill each other. Don't do it. An exception to this rule may be, for example, if you are both coaches. However, you will still have your own unique way of coaching. You will each be better at one area than the other. Administration is a Sacred Gift. Hopefully one of you has it. If not, you need to hire someone to handle it for you. Delegating is a great practice to get into. Resist the urge to do it all yourself just to save a buck. Focusing on the things you enjoy and are gifted at will greatly enhance your productivity.

Sit down and make a list of all the tasks you need to manage. Then, decide who will be in charge of what. If you both feel you are good at the same task, then decide who enjoys doing it more, and agree that's who will be the leader of that category. That which you love to do the most, you will be the best at. Do what you each love and do best, and delegate the rest.

You need to trust one another with your individual brilliance to be able to handle the task at hand. Mistakes will occur. That's how we learn and grow. "Correct and continue" is a good motto. Never fall into the blame game or it will contaminate your relationship. Be very aware of the attitude you have and the language you use with your partner. It's easy to become careless when dealing with those with whom we are close to. When you feel agitated, ask yourself before speaking, "How would I speak to her if she were a colleague in a regular office environment?" Give your beloved business partner the same courtesy, and expect the same from her. It's a simple matter of professional ethics and respect. You each deserve the same consideration you would expect in any other professional environment.

I am a certified facilitator in a process my friend Monique MacDonald created, called *Discover Your Sacred Gifts*. These gifts are all listed in the bible and until she created this incredible workshop most of the information on Sacred Gifts was connected to religion. Monique took the religion out of it so the Discover Your Sacred Gifts process resonates and communicates to people of all belief systems. Basically, as human beings, our beingness doesn't change. It is who we are at birth. Through life experience, our humanness goes through many changes and our personality develops. Each one of us is born with Sacred Gifts which were there at birth and always will be. These gifts are abilities which we feel compelled to do for the benefit of others. This part is key. We may be gifted at something, but if we only do it for ourselves, it's not a Sacred Gift. For example, you may be gifted at making things with your hands, but only do it at home for your own pleasure. In this case, it's a gifted talent, but not a Sacred Gift. If you feel compelled to create for others, you have the Sacred Gift of Craftmanship.

There are 24 primary Sacred Gifts, and on average, we each have around 5 or 6 of them. The *Discover Your Sacred Gifts* workshop was one of the most enlightening workshops I have experienced. It gave me insights on how and where to direct my energy to fulfill my purpose. It freed me to let go of some of the things I thought I should be doing and delegate them to those who have the gifts I lack. Some gifts I knew about, others were a surprise and I didn't even realize were gifts. This is quite common because our Sacred Gifts come so naturally to us, we can easily assume everyone does it. Administration is a Sacred Gift and definitely not one of mine. With this understanding, I have found a personal assistant who has both the gift of administration and the gift of assistance. Now I have more freedom to focus on my Sacred Gifts, some of which include teaching, writing, healing and spiritual challenge. As we become clear about our true gifts, we understand where in our business to most effectively direct our energy in order to achieve the utmost success. *Discover Your Sacred Gifts* is included as a module of my coaching programs. I also offer it as an independent workshop. I know both you and your partner will find it to be an exciting and fascinating process. I guarantee you will each receive greater clarity and understanding about yourselves and one another.

Each one of us is a precious gift to this world. When we own this fact and focus our energy on what is uniquely brilliant about ourselves, we feel more fulfilled, more purposeful, and better able to serve in the highest way. Our careers also become a passion and a fun ride. When your career feels this playful, it's an adrenaline rush which feeds the passion in your intimate relationship. What a beautiful cycle to get caught up in. The matching gifts that you and your partner have will define your business. Your opposite gifts will compliment one another and better define your roles. The gifts neither of you have but need, you can delegate to others to free up your time to focus on what you excel at. Playing your roles in this manner can only result in harmony and passionate abundance, in both love and business.

PART FOUR:

WAR AND PEACE

"A woman often seems to test her man's capacity to remain unperturbed in his truth and purpose. She tests him to feel his freedom and depth of love, to know that he is trustable. Her test may come in the form of complaining, challenging him, changing her mind, doubting him, distracting him, or even undermining his purpose in a subtle or not so subtle way. A man should never think his woman's testing is going to end and his life will get easier. Rather he should appreciate that she does these things to feel his strength, integrity, and openness. Her desire is for his deepest truth and love. As he grows, so will her testing."

- David Dieda, "The Way of the Superior Man"

Testing, Testing

"A sense of humor is a major defense for minor trouble."
- Mignon McLaughlin; journalist and author; 1913 – 1983

"All men and women have an equal need for love. When these needs are not fulfilled it is easy to have our feelings hurt, for which we blame our partner."
- John Gray, author

The best advice I can offer you when your woman goes into test mode is to take it with a dash of humor. Just remember, at the heart of it, she just wants to feel your presence. She wants to feel safe and she needs to know she is deeply loved. In these moments of testing, smile to yourself, stand strong and use your breath. The breath is our life force. It is what holds the energy- the spirit within the body. When we stop breathing, the energy leaves and we die.

Breath plays a huge role in many healing modalities. When our breath is shallow, our energy is weakened. When we connect deeply to our breath, fully conscious of its connection to our body, it empowers us. The practice of breathing deeply will help move you into your presence. Try this: take deep but very relaxed breaths in through your nose and out through your mouth. You want to draw in more breath than usual, but it should not feel like work; just relaxed, deep and easy breaths, in and out. Try practicing this on your own while really feeling the breath in your body. The deeper and fuller your breath, the more energy you'll have and the more present you'll feel. Use this as your tool to help you stand in your presence when you feel your woman is testing you. Remember, the chest is the heart center and the solar plexus the emotional center. These are both areas where our breath enters into our body. When something distasteful comes at you, such as a complaining partner, a natural response is to buckle under to protect this part of your body. However, this type of contraction takes you out of your presence and makes you appear weak.

The best way to earn respect is through kindness, compassionate expression, and humble confidence. It's very difficult to push back against a person who is strong in these areas. Hold your shoulders back, feel expansion in your chest and your belly, stand strong with your feet rooted to the ground, and, for goodness sake, breathe! Consciously connecting your breath to your body creates a deeper connection of your spirit to your physical being. You will feel the strength of your presence as you do this and your woman will feel it in your body language. See past the complaint while standing in this presence and, without words, looking into her eyes, feel the kindness inside of you. Do not take her complaint personally; rather, feel compassion for whatever pain has put her in this mood. Feel all the love you have and breathe freely while holding this connection. She will feel your presence in this moment and she will feel your love.

When a woman tests you and complains, she is trying to distract you from your truth. Most likely she is not trying to distract you from your truth on a conscious level, however that's likely what she's doing. She would much rather feel that she cannot do this than have you weaken and succumb to it. When you stand strong in your truth while continuing to love her, she will feel your strength and, though she may even be a little annoyed at the moment, it will be very attractive to her. By expressing your kindness and compassion you become nurturing. Since women are nurturers by nature, it is a beautiful gift when we feel that in our man as well.

It may feel like this is all some sort of game playing, but it's really not. Remember, providing safety is a quality of the Divine Masculine, so we women are often concerned about our safety, even if it's on a subconscious level. We need to know we are safe in order to let go. If you cannot stand in your truth, we don't feel safe enough to trust, surrender control, and open up completely to you.

I love to dance. It's a great passion of mine. I love free-form dance and I love to dance with a partner. It's a special treat when I get to share the dance floor with a man who knows how to gently take control so I can feel his presence and surrender to his lead. I know I can trust him enough to let go with abandon as he guides me into a dip and feel confident that my head won't come crashing down on the floor. When I experience such a powerful presence, it's like coming home. It's ecstasy to be able to completely surrender to a man who knows his purpose and stands strong in his presence while freely showing his love. When I am feeling cranky and this same man stands before me, strong in his warrior presence and soft in his heart, I feel divinely powerless and safe to fall completely into my feminine presence. Try as I may, I cannot remain cranky.

"The ultimate measure of a man is not where he stands in moments of comfort and convenience, but where he stands at times of challenge and controversy."
- Martin Luther King Jr.

In February 2010, I went on a trip to Costa Rica. The beauty of this land is incredible. I decided to visit an isolated center in the middle of the jungle. The only way to get there is by boat or a hike through the jungle. The boat was needed for an emergency due to the recent rainfall, so we hiked in. In dry weather this hike would take an hour and a half. It took us almost three and a half hours. We had to cross a small channel which was normally very shallow, but had filled and become a river to the height of my chest. It had a strong current we had to fight to get across while holding knapsacks over our heads. The usual path had completely flooded and become a swamp, forcing us to find another route. Sometimes we would sink up to our knees in mud. One woman's credit card washed from her pocket and out to sea. Yes, Mother Nature tested us that day. There were seven of us, all women; six visitors and our guide. Would we have preferred dry weather and a dry path to walk on? Absolutely, but that's not what we found.

Every one of us chose to look past the discomfort we encountered. We moved forward through the soggy jungle, breathing in every fragment of beauty we came across. We gave thanks for every burst of sunshine which broke through the clouds, seeing the lush richness of Mother Earth- the Goddess Gaia all around us. The more we looked for her beauty, the more we saw. My friend with the lost credit card chose to see the humor in her inconvenience, rather than tightening up from it. We were all uncomfortable with these challenges, but we all chose to look at it with amusement and to see past the discomfort and to breathe in the beauty before us.

The most beautiful and alluring quality of the feminine is radiance, that light which glows from within the woman. The more loved she feels, the brighter this light becomes. It is captivating and irresistible. To entice the radiance out of your woman, you must hold fast to your truth, your authentic presence, and let her feel the depth of your love. When you look beyond her testing and look for the beauty of her in that moment, you draw more of it out of her.

Be playful. Do what you can to make her laugh- within reason. Having someone working too hard to nudge a smile when you're feeling cranky can be downright annoying. So practice common sense and intuition. In some cases silence and presence alone are the best response. Complaints are an emotional reaction to whatever is really bothering her. I know we are a confusing breed. Let her know you hear her just by being present for her.

Women need to be seen and heard. If she wants to vent, let her vent. It's her way of releasing stress. I watched a video on YouTube of relationship expert John Gray explaining that when women are stressed they have eight times more blood flow than men to the part of the brain where emotional memories are stored. So her stress actually stimulates the memories of all those things that went wrong in the past, so it can then protect her from what may go wrong in the future. Her ability to talk while someone else listens is what calms down her emotional stress. All she needs you to do is to hold space for her and listen. Mr. Gray also explains that a man's stress center is twice as big as a woman's. It is wired up to the action part of the brain, so it's natural that you want do something and solve the problem. Do not feel you have to solve anything. It won't work and trying will only leave you frustrated. Then your energy will drop as well as your testosterone levels. The talking is simply an energy release for her. The best way to help her, is to offer your presence. Just connect with her and let her vent. Say nothing. Do not try to analyze her feelings; it cannot be done and you will solve nothing. Her feelings are not logical, they are emotional.

"The feminine's moods and opinions are like weather patterns. They are constantly changing, severe and gentle, and they have no single source...

...When a woman gets emotionally intense, a mediocre man wants to calm her down and discuss it, or leave and come back when she is "sane". A superior man penetrates her mood with imperturbable love and unwavering consciousness."

- David Dieda, "The Way of the Superior Man"

"To know when to come closer and when to go away is the key to any lasting relationship."

- DOMENICO CIERI ESTRADA, MEXICAN WRITER

Time Out

Sometimes the best way to restore peace of mind when things get too fired up is to take time out. I don't suggest walking away from your partner and leaving a trail of dust from the anger. This can leave the energy hanging in the air like a bunch of disconnected electrical wires flailing around, clashing into one another. You can't accomplish much all fired up and disconnected. What I do suggest is taking a moment to breathe. Connect with her and calmly tell her that it's important for you to sort this out, but right now you need to take time out, clear your head and get some fresh air. Remember, as long as she feels your presence, she will respect you, even if at that moment she doesn't like you. Anger is a natural human emotion. It is not to be judged. There are ways to release it without hurting yourself or anyone else. High energy sports are great for this, a good workout at the gym, beating the crap out of a pillow, finding an isolated space to let out a good loud scream. There are many ways to release your anger without lashing out at the one you love, thus hurting her and yourself in the process. Take some time out to center yourself. Once you've both had time to sort through things on your own, come back together to discuss the issue with a clear head and calm emotions.

An effective way to make this time out work to your best advantage is to plan it in advance. Arrange in advance to agree to disagree and take time out to catch your breath whenever you have a disagreement that becomes too intense. Agree to resume once you've both had a chance to calm down to a place where you can have a discussion instead of a blame session. Being business partners requires spending an incredible amount of time together.

You need a break once in a while, no matter how much you're in love. When a disagreement gets too intense, time out can be your best option. Just honor and respect the process and one another. Make eye contact and connect with her, and be sure leaving the room and taking space is okay with her in that moment as well. Otherwise you run the risk of contributing to a feeling of abandonment. Be sure there is a mutual agreement and understanding that you are both just taking time to breathe, and you will resume again shortly.

As you feel yourself cooling down, take the opportunity to consider her perspective. Maybe you'll find yourself agreeing with her- or not. At least by giving yourself time to ponder while in your own space, you can come back together to express your viewpoint with greater clarity and without ego running the show.

Once you've had your space, you may come to the realization that your opinion was not the best one. It is very important to take responsibility and ownership of this. Holding on to the need to be right over the need to be happy is destructive behavior. It's an act of maturity and integrity to come clean and admit when you have made a mistake. If you mess up, fess up. It instills a deeper sense of respect and trust, something both you and she must agree to follow through on.

Blame is a destructive action of the ego and serves nothing. Mistakes and poor judgment are tools for learning and growth. As you support one another through this process, you take your consciousness to a higher level and your business grows and expands along with you. Don't let go of that fire altogether, however. Make up sex can be especially hot. Transform that intense energy into sexual passion and fire up the bedroom. Now that's what I call effective energy conversion.

"To silence another, first be silent yourself."

- Latin Proverb

The Art *of* Listening

Shamanism is a beautiful aspect of my personal spiritual practice. I basically live a Shamanistic Tantric lifestyle. It's common practice in Shamanic ceremony, when gathering in circle for a discussion, to do so with a talking stick. Only the person holding the stick has the right to speak. Everyone else must sit in silence and listen until the person speaking feels complete. The Shamanic Priestess Process was a year and a half of intense processing and growth, as myself and my Priestess sisters consistently gathered together for four days at a time, doing very deep work. In my Priestess circle, sometimes the speaking could get pretty heated. Just because we gathered in the name of sisterhood and spiritual consciousness, doesn't mean we didn't get set off by one another from time to time. The love we share is strong, so it didn't happen often. However, put a group of women together long enough and, no matter how enlightened they are, there are bound to be moments when emotions flair, especially when in the midst of doing deep inner work. Learning to own those triggered moments as our own projection of something which is actually unsettled within ourselves is all part of the process. The purpose of the Priestess Process is to help us step into our power as women and serve from a place of passion and compassion; from love and support. This initiation inspired me to facilitate my own circles and share conscious communication with others. When we are set off by those we love and choose to deal with it from our higher selves, free of defensiveness, magic can happen.

Try the practice of the talking stick. Discuss this with your partner and plan to use it as a method of communication. This is one of the most powerful methods you could ever use to communicate and clear the air with one another. Be careful not to fall into the blame game. If the other pissed you off, share how this made you feel, rather than point a finger in blame. You don't have to use a stick. You can use a rock, a piece of jewelry, a ballpoint pen- anything. Let the other speak without interruption. If she wants to spew anger, then let her. Let her say everything she wants to say and unload all the words she needs to unload as you sit in silence, just holding space. If she appears to ramble, let her ramble. It is her way of getting words out, to help her come to her own realization of what is going on. Really listen to what is being said without reacting to it. Receive it instead. Once again... presence. When it is your turn to speak, you do the same and she must be equally present for you. This is a process. Stay with it.

The talking stick method is a beautiful way to communicate, and it works. Once she feels complete, she passes the stick back to you. Before you speak, take a deep breath and really take in what she said. Notice how it feels in your body. Breathe, feeling the connection of your breath in your body, open your chest and then speak while she sits in silence and receives you. Once you are complete with your sharing, offer the stick back to her. She may respond, or feel complete. If she chooses to speak again, once she is complete, she passes the stick back to you again. Continue with this until each of you feels you have been fully heard and understood by the other. It doesn't matter who goes first. The only rule is that whoever is holding the talking stick speaks while the other stays silent; no interruption, not one word until the stick is back in your hand.

The talking stick may not always seem like the most practical method of communication in the office space, but I highly recommend practicing it. Don't wait for a dispute. Just give it a try it to get used to the practice of listening in complete silence while the other speaks. The more you practice this, the more you will be used to communicating in this way, with or without a talking stick or a reasonable facsimile. Feel the emotion behind the words. That's where the real truth lies. If her sharing shows up in the form of complaining then remember, often what we complain about is not the real core issue, but rather a symptom.

When in a dispute, talking over each other accomplishes nothing. This method of sitting in silence and truly listening until there are no words left is a powerful way to fully listen to one another and resolve your issues in a conscious manner. It is a method of communication true to the peaceful warrior.

I have other communication methods I teach couples in my coaching programs. These methods are very effective in helping each of you to be fully seen and heard. If you'd like me to personally guide you through the process, it would be my honor. In the event I am not available, I can recommend you to someone who practices the same method. In the meantime, the talking stick is a simple and effective practice to incorporate into your relationship.

Take advantage of time alone to be silent and to meditate. Being still with your own company and quieting your thoughts will bring you closer to your truth than any task or chore which may need to get done. The mind is a beautiful computer. It stores information and keeps us safe, but we have to remind it that it is here to serve us, not the other way around.

Here is a simple meditation which only takes a few minutes. It's perfect to quiet that run away chatter in your head and go within so you can listen to your own heart beat. It forces your mind to shut down and quiet as you connect to your body and your truth. It's wonderful to practice just before entering a business meeting, when you're feeling overwhelmed, or just have a desire to be still inside. Here it is:

- Sit or lay down so your body is in a comfortable position.
- Close your eyes and begin to take deep, relaxing breaths. Breathe in deeply through your nose and exhale through your mouth, allowing all of your breath to be released, making more space for fresh new breath to enter.
- Tune into the sound of the breath going in and out of your body.
- Feel your breath filling up inside your body with new energy in, and exhaling old energy out.
- Now on the next exhale, feel your shoulders drop and relax with the breath. Go down your body and relax all your muscles in this way down to your fingers and toes.
- Now place one hand over your heart and feel your heart beating deep in your chest. Really go deep inside your body and feel your heart beating, pumping the blood through you. When we start to grow inside the womb, the first thing to develop is the heart. Everything else grows around it. This is your essence. This is where you find truth.

- Now visualize your breath going in and out of your heart and stay with that.
- Then, once you're ready, open your eyes.
  * When you connect with your breath and your body in this way, your ego mind must shut down. It has no choice. Be still like this, breathing, feeling your body, present in the Now. Savor the stillness and feel the truth of who you are in this moment.

As you do this meditation for the first time, your focus will be interrupted while reading the instructions. After one or two times, you'll be able to follow through on your own and go deep, keeping the connection of breath to body. This is a brief but powerful method of bringing yourself to balance and stillness, and connecting to the true essence which is you.

Share this with your partner. It's perfect to do on your own and beautiful and powerful to share. When you do it together, sit close facing one another. Sitting in a cross legged lotus position is great, but if that's not comfortable for you, sit close together in two chairs with your knees touching. As you begin the breath, do it together, inhaling at the same time, then exhaling at the same time, synchronizing your breath. Then turn your focus within and go through the process. When you are complete, open your eyes, looking into the eyes of the other. The depth of the connection you will both feel in this moment is truly beautiful.

An even better solution than reading the instructions in this book is to allow me to personally guide you through the process. Go to the Product link on my website and purchase the meditation titled, "Opening to Abundance." You can download this and start using it right away, or order the CD to be mailed to you. The first track of this meditation is this exact process. Play the audio, sit back and relax as my voice softly talks you through it, with beautiful shamanic wind instruments playing in the background. This meditation is guaranteed to take you to a place of complete and total relaxation from your head down to your toes. As you continue to listen to the CD, I will guide you to be open to the abundance you desire to flow into your life. This is a beautiful meditation for both you and your beloved to do together. I also guide you on how to breathe the energy of your sexual chakra, which is also your creative force, up your body. As you do this while visualizing what you want to attract into your life as if you are already living it, you will activate your life-force energy to supercharge it into being. Enjoy.

"Don't smother on another. No one can grow in the shade."

- Leo Buscaglia, author, speaker, professor 1924 - 1998

Time Away

No matter how much we are in love with someone, we need to have a break and spend time alone or with friends of our own gender. In fact, it's a huge contributor to the health and well being of a relationship. The truth is, no matter how open you and your woman are with one another, some things are best left to discussions with your male friends and she with her girlfriends. Don't try to make her one of the guys. Remember, she's your friend, yes, but you also want her to be your lover. Support her in spending time with her girlfriends, as you go out and bond with the men. When we gather with our own gender out of love and support, void of gossip and competition, we have an excellent opportunity to connect with our feminine essence. We have issues about our bodies and our feelings which can best be supported by other women- our sisters. We play differently when we are with our sister friends. We get silly, we dance, we cry, we talk, we rant, and that little girl comes out to play. These are all ways to let go of the "stuff" we've accumulated through the week. It encourages our feminine essence to come to the surface, ready to take home to share with our man.

After a long week, you want to let go of work. When your business partner is your love partner, it can be healthy for you to both get a bit of space by doing something separately. A night out with your buddies can be just the thing. Take in some sports, brotherly support, golf, or what ever it is you guys do, to release the stress of the week and shift back into play mode. Male bonding with those you think of as brothers is of great value to your life and your relationship. The key is to only spend time with those of high consciousness and integrity, so you are well served by your time with them.

If either of you find yourselves spending time with friends who spend much of their time complaining or criticizing others, you need to acknowledge how toxic this is to yourselves as well. We can all temporarily become complainers from time to time. I'm talking about chronic negativity. I know it can be difficult to separate yourself from those with whom you've been friends for a while, but sometimes we need to reevaluate our friendships. It doesn't mean we stop loving them. Sometimes distancing ourselves is the best thing we can do. It's quite common to evolve and no longer be in alignment with the friends we've been spending our time with. When we open ourselves up to meeting new people, new wonderful friends always show up. Toxic behavior is draining to be around. If you allow yourself to be drained by those outside of your home, you can't be fully present for yourself, your business, or those inside your home. Sometimes loving from a distance is best for everyone.

Women are gathering in circles at this point in time as never before in history. You see it all over the internet, "Goddess Gatherings," "the Divine Feminine" way. If your partner doesn't have a circle of women friends to connect with and would like to, just do a Google search to look for women's networking events, or Goddess Gatherings in your local community, or to find online groups to connect with. This connection will nurture her and support her in a way that will have a very positive effect on your relationship.

At the women's events I facilitate, we spend time sharing with one another as only women can do. We dance together, support and nurture one another. When a woman is feeling burnt out and stressed, I take her by the hand and revive her juicy radiance, as she comes back into alignment with the truth of who she is as a woman. This kind of sister connection is empowering for women, and it contributes to their relationship with their Masculine partners as well. Should your woman spend time with me, whether it's one on one or at a group event, by the time she comes back home to you, she will be radiant and energized. Go to SensualSage.com, and click on the event link. I would love to meet your Goddess. It can also be arranged for me to come to your town to facilitate an event there.

At my couples retreats you also have the opportunity to spend time alone with the other men and my co-facilitator, while I lead the women in our own space of sharing. It would be a great honor to connect and serve both of you this way.

Sometimes spending time away from one another just to be alone is what you really need. Weaving solitude into the balance of your life is a healthy thing. It gives you an opportunity to go to your quiet place and come back to balance. Then, when you do reconnect with your beloved, you are able to be present for one another more fully. Connecting with nature is a beautiful way to spend this solo time. Mother Earth will always bring us back into balance when we take time to breathe in her beauty; to smell the leaves, feel the wind and sun on our faces, and connect with the water. If you like to take time out to read, make use of your time to read material which is unrelated to business. It will help clear out the mind clutter and contribute to greater clarity once you come back to business again.

Hobbies are a great way to keep balance in your life. If you enjoy working with your hands, do it. Create new things. The physical activity of creating things with your hands also helps quiet the mind and creates a balance between your mental and physical beings. Amazing new ideas can come to you while you're engaged in a physical activity which also stimulates your creative juices, such as wood working and carpentry.

If your partner has hobbies and has been putting them on the back burner, encourage her start up a new project. When you take this solo time for yourselves, you have an even greater appreciation of the time you take out for one another. Hobbies are also wonderful to pass on to your children to keep them stimulated. It instills a great sense of accomplishment for them to create something on their own to show for their effort. Solo time is a treasure to add to your tool box to maintain harmony in both your working and intimate partnership.

Maybe you are one of those couples who love to be with each other all the time and taking time away just doesn't feel necessary to you. I heard an interview the other day with a couple in business together who have had great success, working and living in harmony. They choose to spend all their off time together as a family. They don't feel a need to take time away. If that works for you, wonderful! I have a friend who sometimes chooses to spend a few months away from her partner. They deeply love one another and have a beautiful relationship. She just feels the need for extended periods of time away for herself. They have an agreement and are not only at peace with that, but they really love the arrangement. Imagine the heat in their bedroom when they come back together after an extended period apart!

Just be honest with who you are and what you need to do to feel balanced. If you feel yourself wishing for a break and some time alone or with your friends, acknowledge that. Be honest with one another about what works best for you and come to an agreement that you are both happy with. There is no right or wrong here.

"All work and no play, creates a very dull existence."

\- Taylore Ashlie

Boundaries

You must honor and respect the boundary between business hours and personal time. This is mandatory. Do not talk or discuss business after business hours. I know, that's easier said than done. I get that. It's a natural urge to let business talk leak into the dinner hour, but you have to stay on top of this. Make an agreement with one another that, when one slips up, the other will simply say, "Hey, what are you talking about business for?" Seriously, you've got to have a cut off time. There will always be something to do and the work will never be done. I understand sometimes there are deadlines to meet and you'll run into days when you're putting in overtime. However, you must have a firm division between work hours and family time. Often, when the business is new, you feel a need to prove to yourself that you made the right decision by putting in a lot of overtime. Be careful with this. You have to draw the line at some point. Schedule your private life with the same respect as you schedule your business. It's going to take some discipline, practice, and accountability, but to maintain a thriving love life, you have got to have time for fun and get out to play. Or, staying in to play can be a lot of fun too, especially when there are candles and massage oils involved.

Ask yourself, which would cause more turmoil in your life: losing your business, or losing your relationship? I hope you said your relationship. If your business is more important than your partner, then you don't need to read this book. Move on. Release her so she can find someone who will treat her as a priority, as she deserves. I hope you and your business will live happily ever after. The fact is, businesses can be created and recreated. They are replaceable. The love you share is not. Unless you manage your time with this in mind, your relationship will suffer. Continuously putting in those extra hours at night will not produce a happy ending. You see, there is no end to work. There is always more to be done. When you drive yourself too hard and throw things out of balance, the demise of your relationship results. Yes, it's the worse case scenario. Remember, just as your business needs attention to thrive, your relationship needs attention for love and passion to thrive.

The truth is, when you work wisely as opposed to hard, you don't need all that overtime. When you work at something you love to do, you do it with passion and it feels like fun. Yes, there are always boring aspects, that's where delegating comes in. If your work doesn't feel like fun, then you need to figure out what adjustments you need to make. As you both respect and honor each other's roles in the business, you will be more productive. With quality coaching, training, and time management, you can work wisely, be abundant, and have fun in the process.

You both deserve to be nurtured, loved, and share laughter together. The time you take to do this will give you the fuel you need to be present for the business. Don't make the mistake of thinking that once you get the business to a certain point, then you'll be able to take time out to play. A business is a constant work in progress. You need to balance it with play time *now*. When you make one another a priority, you will both be happier, enjoy greater harmony, your intimacy will heat up and deepen, and abundance will be a natural byproduct.

Often, when we are too close to our own issues, we tend to push too hard to make things happen. It's when we take a step back, clear our heads, and savor time with those we love, that we are able to be more focused and see more clearly. Your clients will feel the difference in your energy as well. People choose do business with others because they like them personally; they like their energy and they like being around them. When choosing a marketing coach team, I had lots of people to choose from. I chose the people I liked personally and whose energy I was attracted to. What makes your clients want to do business with you is not just your products and services, but how they feel about you and about themselves when communicating with you. The more time you spend loving and savoring your beloved, the happier you will be. The more harmony you have in your relationship, the more fun you will be to be around. Your clients will feel this in you. It's a win-win.

So, manage your time wisely. Remember what your priorities are. Go easy on yourself and remember it's an ongoing process. You'll need to stay on top of yourselves with this. Agree to hold one another accountable with regard to your time management. Come to an agreement that the personal relationship is the priority and do what you need to do to make sure it stays that way.

I know I talked about this a bit in the section titled, "The Little People" and I'm going to say it again. If you have children, you have to take time away with just the two of you. Date nights are mandatory. Do not compromise on this. Even if it means going for a two hour walk somewhere alone together. You need time where it is just the two of you, with a strict rule of no business talk. This is so important. You also teach your children by example what to expect in their relationships. Date nights will save your relationship and help you continue to grow more deeply in love with one another. This is as important as paying your bills and buying groceries. It must be a nonnegotiable clause in your partnership. No exceptions. Take time away for some passionate play.

"Most men make the error of thinking that one day it will be done. They think, "If I can work enough, then one day I could rest." Or, "One day my woman will understand something and then she will stop complaining," Or, I'm only doing this now so that one day I can do what I really want with my life.

"The masculine error is to think that eventually things will be different in some fundamental way. They won't. It never ends. As long as life continues, the creative challenge is to tussle, play, and make love with the present moment while giving your unique gift."

- David Deida, "The Way of the Superior Man"

You also need to acknowledge where the boundaries of physical space need to be honored. You must communicate sooner rather than later when you feel your boundaries have been crossed. It's often not done intentionally. However, when your partner in business is also your partner in love it's especially easy to get a little sloppy in the office. Respect one another's space the same way you would a colleague's space in a corporate office. For example, say her desk is closer to the doorway, so on your way out, you start leaving your papers on the corner of her desk. You would not do something like that in any other office environment, so do not do it to her. If she is crossing boundaries in your space, speak up and let her know. The sooner the better, otherwise, irritation will build. Just be honest and calm in your communication.

It all comes down to respect. Honoring boundaries in your communication is also very important. Do not cut one another off or disagree before you have heard each other out. Remember the practice of the talking stick method I shared in sectioned titled *The Art of Communication*. Take the time to listen, even when you initially disagree with her thoughts for the business. Assume her intentions are positive and ask yourself, "What is she trying to accomplish by telling me this?" Then listen to her all the way through. You may surprise yourself and end up agreeing with her plan. If you feel she will cut you off when you share your thoughts, say to her, "before you say no, just hear me out and listen to what I have to say." If she still cuts you off, get out the talking stick, or reasonable facsimile.

Even in business, women will tend to talk about what they *feel* about something. Men are more likely to talk about what they *think* about something. It's another difference between the masculine and feminine. I know this can be frustrating for you at times, as you wish we would just get to the point. We don't mean to be irritating, we're just thinking- or rather feeling things out as women do.

Honoring and respecting boundaries requires direct and honest communication. Speaking up before frustration builds is key here. Have integrity. Speak from a place of love and support, as opposed to blame or defensiveness. It's just the conscious thing to do.

"It is impossible to have a healthy relationship with someone who has no boundaries, with someone who cannot communicate directly, and honestly."
- Robert Burney; author

PART FIVE:
ALIGNMENT

"There's always going to be something else that you desire that is summoning life through you. Accept that and use that knowledge as your reason for slowing up a little bit and smelling the roses a little more, and savoring a little more, and complimenting a little more, and appreciating yourself and others a little more. In other words, just be more of a basker than you are anything else."

- Abraham-Hicks

Dialed In

The method to living a greatly rewarding reality with both our personal and professional lives is simple. Have integrity, do work which you love that benefits others, and always reach for that which feels good. We are only capable of giving off one frequency at any time and there are only two forms to choose from: negative or positive, expansion or contraction. We act from a place of love or we act from fear. Ego debased, or from our higher consciousness. Anyway you say it, it all means the same. What ever frequency we vibrate, that's what we receive. You dial the radio to 87.5 FM, you don't expect to receive 550 AM. It works the same with us. We are living, Source energy beings. Science has proven at the core of our cells, we are pure energy. Every moment of every day, we have a choice about what energy we resonate. Yesterday is gone and tomorrow doesn't exist. The only reality is Now. Whatever signal we put out now is what we will receive next. It's that simple.

So, what frequency is your dial set to? If you don't like the channel, then adjust it or you're just going to keep hearing and receiving the same old, same old. It's your choice. To have harmony in the workplace, you must resonate harmony from within. To have passion in your romance, you must resonate passion from within. To receive love from another, you must resonate love from within. It helps others to love you when you feel a strong healthy love of yourself. After all, how can you expect someone else to do something unless you're willing to do it yourself? To experience a happy life, we need to find things to be happy about. We live on a beautiful planet. We can choose to give our attention to the destruction that makes us feel bad, or we can pay attention to the beauty that makes us feel good. I'm not suggesting you become an ostrich with you head in the sand. It's good to be aware of what's happening on the planet. But when you continuously look for and complain about what is wrong, that will be the frequency you set yourself to, and that will become the channel that will continue to define your life.

There is so much beauty in this world to give our attention to, and miracles happen every day. Be aware of world events, but focus on what makes you feel good. Tune your dial to the good feeling channel. Allow that to be the frequency you vibrate as often as possible, and I assure you more of it will show up. Try smiling, even when you don't have anything to smile about. The cells in your body will respond to the smile, and since the core of our cells we are pure energy, your body's vibration will adjust to the frequency of your smile. Don't believe me? Try it.

It is so important that we only choose careers we love. If we choose something just because we believe it make us a lot of money when our hearts are not into it, we can't be fulfilled. It will feel like a lot more work than necessary, and we'll put ourselves out of alignment from what we are truly meant to do. This is not the path to living up to our purpose.

The more we do what we love, the more we are in alignment with Source- the truth of who we are. For you and your partner to be in alignment and work in harmony, you both have to love what you do. Together, as you each tune into the same channel, you can play the most beautiful music imaginable in both the boardroom and the bedroom.

"Fear, doubt and worry are among the greatest obstacles, not only to success but to happiness as well. Therefore, one of the biggest differences between rich people and poor people is that rich people act in spite of fear, poor people let fear stop them."

- T. Harv Eker, from the book "Secrets of the Millionaire Mind"

Ka Ching Ka Ching

Money is the exchange we receive for our professional services, skills and gifts. Some see it as the root of all evil, others perceive it as the path to freedom. Money is the most frequent subject of conflict within relationships. We can't get away from it. It plays a part in our lives pretty much every single day. We need it to clothe ourselves, to feed ourselves, to provide shelter, heat, communication, entertainment, etc. It's a necessary reality of our physical existence. We must make peace with this thing called money if we want it to be abundant in our lives.

Money is energy. On its own, it simply consists of pieces of paper, metal, or plastic. On the internet, it's not even something we can pick up and touch; it's just numbers on the screen. Try this: rip out a page from a magazine with an image you like, then hold a $20, $50 or $100 bill in the other hand. When you look at the page from the magazine, you may enjoy the image and seeing it may even give you pleasure. Now look at the money. Do you feel a difference? Does it feel cold to you, or do you love the way it feels? Do you feel the power behind it? Can you see the possibilities of what you can exchange it for? Does it feel different to you, the higher the number? It's still just a piece of paper with ink on it.

Coins are just pieces of metal. The difference is the energy you choose to give them. When the energy you place around money is fear based, it creates a sense of coldness. People only fight about money when they fear it will run out or there will not be enough. By shifting this fear based way of thinking and putting the energy of love into money, then the source of the conflict is eliminated.

When we get stuck in the limited thinking that money is scarce and there just isn't enough to go around, or that even if there is enough now, there won't be later, we are allowing ourselves to be controlled by our fear. This same fear is what causes greed. A wealthy man who displays greed was not born that way and the money didn't cause it. It is his fear that he may not have enough later which causes the greed, and the more money he has, the more his greed becomes obvious.

There are many wealthy people who live a life of abundance and do wonderful things with their money to help people. The energy they have around their money is the energy of love. The more money they have, the more their kindness becomes obvious. They understand how the flow of the energy of money works and live in appreciation and respect for it. Oprah is a great example of this. Through her love, she uses her money to create schools in Africa, clothe the children, and provide them with possibilities they might not otherwise have had. Imagine the ripple this love has created, the kind of adults these children will grow up to be, and the changes they will create in the world; all because of one woman's love and compassion. She also loves the luxury it provides for her, and lives in appreciation of that. She knows she is worthy of this luxury. This is all a love based way of *being* around money.

We are all connected to the same love source. Our love is what makes us Divine and what continues to connect us to the Divine. When we put the energy of love into our money, the action connected to it becomes sacred.

Shortly after the earthquake happened in Haiti, I was listening in on a conversation about it at the coffee shop. A man commented on the million dollar contribution made by Angelina Jolli and Brad Pitt. He said, "That's nothing to them, with all the money they have. It's like us giving $1000." I didn't ask, but I'm willing to bet that man did not donate $1000 to the cause. Comments like this pass judgment on money and those who have it. Judgment is fear based and will repel money from coming into your life. The appropriate response would be to praise their generosity and follow their example, even if all you can contribute is the cost of a cup of coffee. When you do it with love, you fuel the energy of money with a positive charge.

We all deserve to live in luxury and there is no limit to its availability. We are the only ones who limit ourselves. When we pass judgment upon those with money, especially those who do good with it, we create an energy around money which prevents it from coming into our lives. We cannot become what we push against. The frequencies don't match up.

"When we change the energy around money from fear to love, we bridge the gap between the material and the spiritual world and make it possible for the unlimited abundance of the Divine to flow freely into our own lives and throughout the world."

- Barbara Wilder, "Money is Love"

The word money comes from the Goddess Juno Moneta. Juno Moneta was the wife of Jupiter and guardian of the finances of Rome. In ancient times, Priestesses were the guardians of the money in the temples, honoring its connection between the Divine and material things. Money was used to exchange and honor the services and skills of people, recognizing these services and skills as Divine gifts and offerings.

Take a close look at your life with your beloved to evaluate how the money energy is flowing in and out of your lives. Take note of where it may be stuck, such as unpaid bills, people who owe you money, not paying yourself regularly. Are you tithing a percentage of your money? Do what you can to keep the energy flowing and circulating. When money comes into your life, take a moment to feel appreciation for it. Recognize that it is the combination of each of your gifts that attract this money. Consciously recognize the sacredness of this. Acknowledge as Divine Beings that your abilities to provide your gift to others create the abundance you desire in this material world.

The Universe has unlimited abundance and we, as extensions of Source energy, are intended to live in abundance. The fastest way to get there is by practicing gratitude and living in love. If you find yourself experiencing tension in your partnership around money, it always comes from a fear-based source. Fear is a money repellant. Fear of money is an illusion and an ego-based reaction. Shift the energy around your money to love and, I guarantee, money will show up much faster with less effort. As you spend money, visualize it helping and serving those who end up with it. Imagine it having a healing effect as it goes out into the world.

"The fear that there is not enough money comes from our separation from the sacred aspect of money. In the divine realm, there is abundance for all. But over the centuries, we have created a world of duality, where the material world and the spiritual world have become separated."

- Barbara Wilder, from the book "Money is Love"

I shared in the section, "The Dance of the Masculine and Feminine" about the effects of adrenaline and oxytocin with regards to attracting prosperity for men and women. This is an important part of the equation, and there are often layers to the story of what can be blocking financial prosperity from coming into a person's life.

For women especially, money can be a very emotional topic. You or your partner may have your own wounds and damaging belief systems around money. If so, I suggest you both work through these problems with regard to your thinking about money. I know for me, I had to overcome boundary and deservability issues. I had a habit of undercharging for my services, and over delivering. I had difficulty saying "no" and was easily swayed to reduce my rates. As a coach, over delivering results in overwhelm for the client. The shadow belief around these issues is fear of rejection, and a belief that other people's desires are more important than you.

Some people have shame connected to money. Some worry that others will not accept or love them if they make more money. There are those dealing with guilt who feel they are not good enough. Some people play it small and believe they are not significant. All of these belief systems are fear-based and are illusions that can be transformed into empowering beliefs. As a Certified Money Marketing and Soul coach, and a Certified Money Breakthrough Method coach, I have powerful systems I use to help people identify exactly what has been blocking them from creating the financial reality they are wanting to create, and quickly eliminate the unconscious emotional junk that has been interfering with creating financial abundance.

Men and women tend to have very different belief systems around money. It goes back to the days of our ancestors. Think about it, what does money represent? Freedom, power, independence, security. Until recent history, women have turned to men for their security.

Let's talk about the power around money. Power has a different meaning for men. You see your target, you aim, and you go for it. You bring home the hunt and you provide. The masculine is the mental and physical energy. You have stronger bodies than women. When we think of power around the masculine, we think of an intellectual and physical nature. When women who are naturally feminine try to become aggressive and powerful the masculine way, it goes against their nature.

Although a woman's power is in her ability to nurture, to serve, and to take care of people, many women rarely think of being financially rewarded for these qualities. If your woman has an inner programming interfering with her ability to make more money, it will help if she acknowledges the value of her nurture instincts. These qualities are connected to her ability to create. As she becomes aware of this, she can own her Divine Feminine power. As she owns her Divine Feminine power and stands in it, she can also own her right to reap financial rewards for her gifts.

You see, many women have been taught to be nice, and not ruffle any feathers. This belief for women goes against the words "stand in your power." By understanding this, you can support your woman in helping her acknowledge her ability to serve, nurture, care for others, and be creative as her power source. As women put value on these qualities, we can come into alignment at the thought of being financially rewarded for them. Rewards also come in many other forms. They come in the form of gratitude expressed by clients, the fulfillment of making a contribution to changing someone's life, and in the form of money.

Most women have a desire to make money. However, their unconscious programming is stronger and pushes down their ability to do so. Part of this unconscious programming is that it's not okay for a woman to make more than a man. This is a controversial statement, but if women look deep inside and tune into their feelings on this, they will find it's true. We have been taught that if we make more money than men, that we will disempower them. The truth is, this is often not how the man feels. It's more of a women's issue. Many men don't have an issue with their woman making more money. This is the unconscious belief system which has been programmed into women's psyche. This shows up because we become concerned about hurting other people's feelings. We prefer having less to worrying about hurting someone by having more. It's silly, I know, but on a subconscious level, this is what is going on with many women. Don't believe me? I'll prove it...

Go to my book website right now at www.ThePlayfulPartnershipBook.com. You will see an offer I created for readers only to opt in and receive a complimentary training video, titled "Secrets for Women to Discover How They Give Up Their Power With Money". Invite your woman to go through the process and support her by listening and being present. Money is a very emotional subject, especially for women. When you tell her about this, or as she reads these words, at first your beloved may not believe this applies to her. However as she does the exercise, it's quite likely she will discover otherwise and be quite surprise by the results. This can be a powerful breakthrough for her and your partnership.

This is one of the processes of the Money Breakthrough Method, created by my mentor Kendall Summerhawk. The Money Breakthrough Method, is powerful and brilliant in the way it releases disempowering beliefs and emotions around money, replacing them with empowering beliefs and actions. Participants experience huge breakthroughs and transformations around their relationship with money. There are also practical systems which they learn to put into place which effectively eliminate debt and create more income.

I offer a six week Money Breakthrough Method virtual workshop, as well as one on one coaching. By signing up on my website, you will be the first to be contacted about any upcoming teleseminars and workshops. So, go to www.ThePlayfulPartnershipBook.com now and receive your free training.

Remember to express gratitude as money comes into your lives. Whatever energy you put into your money, that is the energy you will receive back. If you feel lack, you will end up with lack. If you feel appreciation and love around money, you will receive more of it to love. Spend your money with love. Feel your appreciation and love for yourselves and one another as the money flows in. As you focus your energy in this direction, combined with education, responsibility and inspired action as well as a belief that there is always enough to go around and it will never run out. That is the reality you create.

PART SIX:

EXPAND AND RECEIVE

"The thing about performance, even if it's only an illusion, is that it is a celebration of the fact that we do contain within ourselves infinite possibilities."

- Sydney Smith, English Clergyman 1771 – 1845

"As we express our gratitude, we must never forget that the highest appreciation is not to utter words, but to live by them."

\- John F. Kennedy

Celebrate *and* Appreciate

Everyone wants to feel acknowledged and appreciated. It provides inspiration and incentive to keep us going. What we give our attention to expands every time. The more energy we give to our accomplishments, the more accomplishments we'll have to celebrate. The more attention we give to our problems, the more problems we'll have. I'm not talking about avoiding or shrinking from them. The secret to success is to grow larger than any problem that may present itself in either business or your relationship. One of the best ways to do this is for you and your partner to celebrate your successes at every chance you get. Really big successes like landing the VIP client you were hoping for require a big celebration. However, even the simple stuff you accomplish throughout your day warrants celebration. I recommend doing this at the end of each work day. It can be something as simple as a high five, or a nice juicy kiss. It's a very good way of shifting out of work mode and into some passionate playtime.

If your team extends beyond the two of you, celebrating the success of your staff will dramatically increase their productivity. Acknowledging and appreciating them for even the simplest tasks will inspire greater performance, loyalty, and a desire to please. Celebrating success plays a huge role in a smooth operating team and is a key element of strong leadership. Your business depends on the two of you fully showing up to get the job done and never taking one another for granted.

It's not enough to just speak the words. Appreciation of one another must be prevalent in your actions. If you really want to amp up the passion in your life, praise your woman and praise her often. Vocalize the beauty you see in her, deep from within your heart. Praise her in the way she moves, the way she looks, her scent, the sound of her voice. Let her feel your love and admiration for her in the way you give to her. Remember, the woman is the reciprocator. Every woman loves to feel cherished. The more cherished she feels, the more she will give back. If you are not feeling appreciated by her, then speak up. Ask her, "What do you appreciate about me?" Her silence doesn't mean she doesn't feel it. Sometimes, just like you, we can get preoccupied and forget to say what we're feeling in our hearts. We always love to receive what we are willing to give and when we don't, the one doing all the giving eventually feels drained, straining the relationship.

A beautiful way to show appreciation and to celebrate one another through actions is by offering gifts. Gift giving for no other reason than just to say "I love and appreciate you" will always inspire a beautiful response. It doesn't have to be extravagant. A single rose will do the trick. Of course, a little extravagance now and then is always nice too.

Neither of you want to make the mistake of assuming the other knows they are appreciated without speaking and expressing through your actions. Making assumptions can, more often than not, lead to regret. I know I've gotten myself into a pickle or two just from assuming someone was on the same page as I was, only to find out we were reading entirely different books.

"Assumptions are termites of relationship."
- Henry Winkler

"Just imagine the day that you stop making assumptions with your partner and eventually with everyone else in your life. Your way of communicating will change completely, and your relationships will no longer suffer from conflicts created by mistaken assumptions."
- Don Miguel Ruiz, "The Four Agreements"

Expressing appreciation for one another on a regular basis is also an act of kindness and awareness. Practice it always with your loved ones, your staff, clients, and even the cashier at the grocery store. You will experience a flow of ease and harmony, just by being consistent with this simple practice. When we are kind, we attract peace of mind.

"In Avatar, *both the male and female are leaders, each with unique powers and dignity. They cooperate for the good of each other and all. In order for this to take place, we must first tell a story of the beauty and value of each gender. They must be equally valued for their empowerments and skills."*

- JEFFREY ARMSTRONG,

QUOTE FROM HIS BOOK "SPIRITUAL TEACHINGS OF THE AVATAR"

WWW.SPIRITUALTEACHINGSOFTHEAVATAR.COM

"Life is supposed to be fun."

- Abraham-Hicks

White Water Wisdom

During my trip to Costa Rica I discovered I have a passion for white water rafting. I rafted down the Pacuare River twice while there. This is said to be the most beautiful river in the world. I believe it. While rafting, it occurred to me that we must move through life the same way we moved down that river. I once heard an audio of Abraham-Hicks comparing how we need to travel through life like a white water rafting experience. I understood it then, but there's nothing like the actual physical experience to really feel it on a cellular level.

It is obvious the only way to go is downstream. Paddling upstream would be foolish. There were times when the rapids were fierce and everyone in our raft had to paddle hard and work together in complete synchronicity or the current would work against us and we'd flip over. When one of us fell out, we all stuck together and paddled toward the rescue and pulled the person back in. Before and after a rapid, there were always moments of calm, allowing us to relax our paddles and breathe in the beauty around us. Sometimes we even got to jump overboard and play in the water or just lay back and float with the soft current. It was divine as the giant blue butterflies flew past and the gentle waterfalls flowed into the water around us, pouring down from the black rock canyon. After these sweet breaks, we would climb back aboard the raft and get back to work as the river built up its speed again.

It was imperative throughout the entire journey that we listen to our guide and do exactly what he said, when he said it. As long as we did that, we were safe and the ride was beautiful, exhilarating, peaceful and full of laughter.

Just like life, the obstacle that often comes hand in hand with a white water raft trip, is the fear of falling. During my second white water raft trip on the Pacuare River I did fall. I did more than fall, I was thrown way off course up and out of the raft, then went falling into the river. When I first got tossed from the raft, I didn't even realize it was happening. I was paddling vigorously, looking at the white froth beneath me wondering why I could not feel the tension of the water on the paddle. It felt like an out of body experience. Next thing I knew, I was flat on my back in the water. I remembered the training they gave me and crossed my arms on my chest and then looked around for my raft. It was approximately 15 feet behind me. I met up with the raft and my team pulled me back on board. I realized in that moment that the experience I feared the most about the journey was actually quite exhilarating and a fun contribution to the experience.

Often that which we fear the most, is not fearful at all, and in fact, it can enhance the journey we are on. It's in those moments of falling or feeling tossed off of our path when we can receive the big *ahah* moments. Most often the thing we fear is the unknown, something that we have not experienced yet, therefore an illusion. When you have a great support team, whether that support team consists of your beloved alone, or a staff as well, there will always be someone to pick you up when you fall, and to bring you back on course. It is in those moments when precious transformations can happen.

Think of your life as a white water rafting trip. Always take the path of least resistance, because trying to go upstream is not the wise man's method of moving forward. Sometimes the waters will be rough and you and your beloved will have to work hard as a team to get through it. If one of you leaves the other struggling on their own, you both suffer. If one of you falls, the other must be there to pull them back up. If you stick with it and work together, you'll get through it and make those moments of calm all the sweeter. Take time to watch the butterflies and fully appreciate the beauty along the way. When you work together in harmony, it will be an exhilarating ride, laced with serenity and unexpected pleasures. And, you have got to listen to your guidance. You have an inner knowing within you; that gut feeling, intuition, your higher self- whatever you want to call it, trust it. Listen to your guidance. It's there to serve you and will never let you down. The more you listen, the easier it is to hear it and the more you will learn about yourself and one another.

If you've never gone white water rafting, I highly recommend it. It is exhilarating ride and a beautiful metaphor on life.

PART SEVEN:

THE SHIFT

"A woman must be able to trust you to take charge if she relaxes her own masculine edge. This is true financially, sexually, emotionally, and spiritually. The man doesn't have to actually do all the work, but he must be able to steer the course if his woman is going to relax into her feminine without fear."

– David Dieda; The Way of the Superior Man

"It's alright letting yourself go, as long as you can get yourself back."

- Mick Jagger; The Rolling Stones

From Warrior *to* Goddess

So, business hours are over. You've created your living space into your own little sanctuary. The office is out of site. The two of you are out of your professional clothes and ready to relax and enjoy some time off. How do you make the shift? Your woman has been in work mode, connected to her masculine essence of focus, making decisions, and taking action. How do you help shift her back? I'm going to share something based on a true story which I heard from a friend. He understood the dynamics of masculine and feminine energy and the importance of shifting her into her feminine essence to enjoy a delicious night of romance. This is a beautiful story and a brilliant idea, so take notes. I don't remember all the details, so I'll elaborate a bit. He spent two weeks planning it and, according to him, the rewards were perfection.

It was their 17th wedding anniversary. He purchased 17 roses. He laid out just one rose in plain view where it would be the first thing she saw when she came home. There was a note attached to the rose that read, "Go to the kitchen and enjoy a glass of wine." She went to the kitchen and there was a glass freshly poured, with another rose next to it with a note. It said, "Now go to the bedroom, get out of your work clothes and put on your robe." She went into the bedroom where her robe was laid out. There was another rose and the note said, "Go soak in a bubble bath." Next to the candle-lit bubble bath was another rose. (A trail of rose petals leading the way and sprinkled in the bath would be a nice touch.) This note said, "Go to the bedroom and put on your dress." She went to the bedroom and there was her favorite dress laid out on the bed. (If you buy her a new one, be sure that it will be a perfect fit and she will love it, otherwise she will have to choose another.) Step by step he relieved her of every decision she could make right down to the dress, the jewelry, her make up- everything! By the time she got to rose #17, and went downstairs to meet him where he was waiting for her in a stretch limo, she was so fully in her feminine essence, the radiance of her lit up the entire street. The rest of the night flowed effortlessly. I can guarantee that few women can resist being sexually responsive to such a beautiful set of events. I'm willing to bet that night was one of the most passionate of their marriage.

Obviously, this was a very special occasion and it took him two weeks of creative planning to pull it off. I understand it's not practical to plan something so extravagant every week. If you do plan such an event, it will be a night your beloved will never forget and it will reinforce the depth of your love for her. The point is to do what it takes to help her let go of the masculine essence she has in business mode and to bring her back to her feminine. Women love to know that we are seen and heard. Men do too, but remember the woman is the receptor. It is the nature of the feminine to receive what is being presented; then she responds and gives back accordingly. Look at how our sexual organs are designed. Ours go within and receive. Your genitals protrude and reach outside of your body.

Reach out to her, take initiative, and instill confidence in her that you are in control and she is relieved of all responsibility. She will then be in a place where she can relax and trust that everything will be okay. When she is in this state she can be more receptive. Your presence will be more visible to her; she will notice and you will feel more seen and heard, too. When you do not take the lead, you're putting her in the driver's seat. When she is in control and making decisions, she is incapable of fully falling into her feminine essence. Take the time to hold space for her this way and I promise you, her radiance will shine through and the rewards will be worth the effort.

I know after a hard day at work you may be tired and just want to let go yourself. Sometimes you won't have the energy to make much of an effort at anything. Just the simple act of curling up on the sofa in one another's arms and holding her for a little while, letting her melt into your warmth and feeling your strength, will help her let go of any control she's been holding on to and bring her back into her softness.

As the two of you become more aware of this dynamic with your masculine/feminine energy, you can make the shift as quick as a snap of your fingers. When business is up and everything is exciting, or even when you are experiencing challenges, you will be tempted to keep talking about work when trying to move into private time. I can be a bit of a chatter box when I get excited about my new endeavors. When your woman falls into chatter mode just as you're ready for love, look deep into her eyes and show her your love. Gently caress her, kiss her, and remind her that it's time to shift. Let her feel your strength, your love, your romantic touch, and the softness of your voice. As her heart softens, her mind will quiet, making it easy to surrender to your wooing.

If your mind is distracted, constantly going into business mode, turn to your woman. Look at her. See her beauty. Touch her and kiss her. With your ability to single focus, you simply have to make the effort to shift your focus from business to her. Close your eyes and feel your breath in your body to quiet your mind and make the shift more effectively.

Some days you will be fired up with adrenalin. Maybe you landed that big client you had been hoping for. You try but you can't shut down that busy head of yours. Maybe it's from things going really well, or maybe it's from over stress. How do you quiet it down? Well, a great way to burn through excess energy is to ride the wave with high outbursts of energy. You can go take it out in a squash court or a good hard run. If you have anger attached to this excess energy, lingering from a bad day at the office, sports is a wonderful way to get it out of your system. However, if it's simply a matter of fired up adrenaline needing a creative release, I have another suggestion.

It's important when going in this direction that you and your partner are in agreement. This agreement can be verbal, or through eye contact. Just be sure it exists. Now, tap into that animalistic, hungry primal energy inside of you. Look into the eyes of your woman, be in your presence, and let her feel the passion in you. Letting her see how much you want her, take her, kiss her with hunger, giving her all you have, spilling all your excess energy into primal sex as you devour and savor every inch of her. Consistently make eye contact so she can see her beauty and your love in your eyes. Be vocal without holding back, Letting out screams is an incredible way to release energy when indulging in sexual activity. Take the time to satisfy and take her to complete climax before taking orgasm for yourself. This does not work if it is a selfish act. Stay very aware of her boundaries and just let go. The secret here is balance. Women love slow, sensual, romantic tenderness. However, outbursts of primal sex are also very hot as long as she still feels safe, loved and physically fulfilled.

Once your excess energy has been released through this primal expression, then I recommend shifting into a gentle, tender, beautiful finish. The occasional adrenaline rush can be fun for women, as long as it is accompanied with a conscious awareness of safety and she can quickly go from there to a place of feeling loved and nurtured. In the upcoming section of this book, titled "Ecstasy," I go into a more detailed description of love-making through the practice of Sacred Tantric sexuality. You will discover how to connect more deeply, open your woman up to receiving you more fully, and how to experience ultimate Divine Union in the art of love making. So, keep reading. You're almost there, but first a very important piece to the equation....

"If you cannot face directly your sexuality, you will never discover your true spirituality"

-White Tigress Manual

Herstory

I'd like to share some history of the feminine, which I like to refer to as herstory. An awareness of this can help you better understand your woman, and how together you may heal some wounds she may be carrying around her sexual energy. At least one out of every four men reading this book will be with a partner who has experienced some form of sexual abuse. You may have even been a victim yourself. We are not only affected by the experiences of our past in this lifetime, but the accumulated experiences of society as a whole. As we take a closer look at the big picture and how it has unfolded through time, it's easier to see our own big picture.

There was once a time when the spiritual gathering places were Priestess temples. These Priestesses were the healers, nurturers, and confidants of the community. They understood the integral connection of sexual and spiritual energy and honored it as a sacred gift from the Divine. Priestess temples were eventually destroyed and churches were built on top of the land where temples once stood. Women were then forbidden to practice medicine and eventually the witch burnings began. Women felt forced to point fingers and blame one another out of fear for their own lives. If they showed even the slightest sign that they enjoyed sex, they were accused of consorting with the devil. Women with land were in the most in danger. One man was employed to search them out, others to arrest them, others to possess their land. The land and property was sold and everyone shared in the profits. Witch burning was a big business, and it went on for 300 – 400 years. Yet it is barely mentioned in the history books.

For a couple of thousand years, the patriarchal religions have worked to split our sexuality from our spirituality. We became sexually repressed. Guilt and shame were cast upon the very energy which makes it possible for us to exist and make the journey from the spiritual realm into this physical experience. Since then, the only female sexual role models have been the Virgin and the whore, with nothing in between. We were either a "good girl" or a "bad girl." This is a wound which has been passed on from mother to daughter for generations.

Our bodies are created so perfectly, so magnificently. The clitoris is the only human body part in creation which has the sole purpose of pleasure. It is no coincidence that the orchid flower resembles the sex of the woman. It comes in a variety of shapes, sizes and colors and is so delicate and so precious. It must be handled with great care and respect in order to flourish. What an incredible gift this is, such a delicate part of the female anatomy and yet so powerful. In the practice of Sacred Tantric sexuality, the vagina is referred to as the Yoni, meaning "sacred space." This acknowledges that it is where life- creation- begins. The penis is the Lingam, meaning "wand of light." When a man enters a woman, honoring her in every way from a place of love, the Lingam can be a source of great light and warmth inside her dark, mysterious sacred space. When the opposite of this energy takes place, the result is darkness and pain. It rips a wound in our soul and disempowers both men and women. The Patriarch became fearful of the great power of women's sexual energy and thus repressed it. Genital mutilation, which most commonly takes place in Africa, is one result of such repression. This repression has left a huge scar on society as a whole.

The Priestess archetype is found in all religions throughout time, yet has been lost in our psyches for the past few thousand years. The word Priestess now sounds a little too woo-woo for many people. However, the definition is not. All women have a Priestess within them. I am an initiated Shamanic High Priestess. What does this mean? A Priestess is a woman in service, a woman who holds the wisdom of the connection between the Spiritual realm and Mother Earth, who longs to express herself in the temple of her life. She is a woman trained in performing sacred ceremonies. A Priestess is dedicated to life affirming values. She empowers, teaches, and guides change on all levels. A Priestess walks the feminine path of self care, beauty, and sacred sexuality.

I went through a year and a half of extensive journeying with my circle of women, which was facilitated by Anyaa McAndrew, a High Priestess and Bishop in the Madonna Ministry. We explored the deepest part of ourselves. We looked our shadows in the face and loved them regardless of their darkness and, in so doing, held them in the light, making them powerless. We made a conscious connection between our spiritual paths, our political beliefs, our sexuality, and our money stories. Through the Priestess process, I became an ordained Minister in the Madonna Ministries. Now I incorporate my wisdom and the knowledge I learned on this journey, as well as in life, to guide men and women to step fully into their own light. I consider it a great honor. "Priestess consciousness teaches us to live our lives in a sacred way in service to the world, while shamanic consciousness teaches us about the natural cycles of death and rebirth, shadow and light, human and divine."

"Every woman regardless of her level of spiritual development, has an inner patriarch who sets limits, and boundaries for her. How well our inner patriarch assists us in standing as co-creators with Spirit and expressing our essence qualities depends entirely on how we work with it in transformational ways."
- ANYAA MCANDREW, WWW.GODDESSONTHELOOSE.COM

It was through Anyaa's teachings that I learned about the inner patriarch inside of women, also known as the super ego or inner critic. When women come together in groups, they can sometimes take on characteristics which could be described as downright vicious, back-biting, and undermining. When women project their judgments on other women, it is often the unhealthy patriarchal energy inside of us. At the same time this energy represses and denies the woman's inner essence. This results in a split between the inner feminine and the inner masculine. When this happens, the heart energy becomes blocked and women project the patriarchy onto one another.

This is why, when I work with women, I start by helping them connect with the masculine inside themselves. We identify it and then I guide them to transform the patriarch into the healthy Divine Masculine who witnesses without judgment. This then transforms lack of worth to worthiness. When they do this, they feel safe in their own bodies, which in turn makes it possible for them to fully express their Divine Feminine aspect for themselves and toward one another. As they connect with the healthy masculine within themselves, they also become more in alignment with that energy in their beloved- in you.

Shame and guilt originated in patriarchal societies and continues due to a lack of consciousness. Shame and guilt over our sexuality has infected us and has disempowered men and women alike. This is in no way a judgment on men. I love your beautiful selves. We have all been victims of this damaging history and herstory. By recognizing this and going to the source, we can cast a light on this shadow aspect, and transform how we feel about ourselves and how we view others. It's time to acknowledge and remember that our sexuality is integrally connected to our spiritual self, that it is our creative force and to honor it as a gift from the Divine. As we do this, we are empowered and we step into wholeness as Divine beings in physical bodies.

Remember when you were a young boy entering puberty? Were you taught how to honor this beautiful sexual energy of yours, the sacredness of it? Were you taught how to honor the Divine in the girls you thought about or had sexual relations with? Or, were you made to feel shameful if you were caught touching your own genitals? You can see it today still showing up in boys as they disrespect girls they have sex with. They put girls in two categories, the good ones and the bad ones. Those so called "bad" girls just want to be loved. This is true of adults as well.

In my experience, at the core of all wounds is a little girl or boy not knowing they are "good enough." They do not recognize how Divine they really are and just want to give love and be loved. When boys and men disrespect girls and women in this way, they are also disrespecting the feminine energy within themselves. If you are a parent or planning to be, you want to pay especially close attention to this. It's so important that your son or daughter recognize they are a Divine being and recognize this in others as well. The further away a person appears on the surface from being Divine, the deeper their pain. As we understand and see this, we open ourselves up to greater compassion. And the world, one person at a time, becomes a more harmonious place in which to exist.

An African woman named Efua Dorkenoo, author of "Cutting the Rose," has brought great awareness to the subject of female genital mutilation. She shares stories of the old days from her great-grandmother in Zambia about how, when the girls entered puberty, they were taken into huts for two weeks and taught how to honor their bodies by the women elders. They were taught everything about their sexuality. They were given wooden models to practice on. The elders would lie on top of the girls and pretend to be the man, teaching them how to move their hips and adopt the best positions for the most pleasure. At the end of the two weeks when these girls returned to the community they felt special, honored and had a clear understanding of their sexual energy and how to honor it. Dorkenoo explains that girls who are given this kind of education at puberty tend to exude a confidence in themselves and a deep respect for their own sexuality. She says, "It gives them a sense of power which they are taught not to abuse. These girls don't tend to be promiscuous. Sexuality is their gift from God. They may flaunt it in the way they walk, but they will save the best of what the elders have taught them for their man."

I don't expect you to call upon the grandmothers of your children and have them do the same, but imagine what a difference it would make if all young people were educated about sexuality in an open and a truthful manner. In the movie Avatar, the women were practically nude, yet there was nothing exploitive about the way they were portrayed. Both the men and women lived and worked together in harmony, honoring the role they each played, connecting all that is physical to the Divine. They were conscious of all their actions, both in the present and the future, and how they affected each other. This way of "being" touched everyone who saw this movie, because deep in our core, we know this is how it should be. This is the path of living a Sacred Tantric Lifestyle.

I'd like to share a bit of my personal herstory with you. One reason I was drawn to be a Cuddle Party facilitator is because the workshop teaches not only proper communication and honoring boundaries with regard to touch, but the ability to say "no" and be comfortable using "no" as a complete sentence. When saying "no" feels difficult, it's because we feel a need to explain our "no," or we worry about hurting the other person's feelings. Saying "no" was something I was incapable of as a young girl and teenager and have since discovered I share this with many girls and women. I acknowledge that men also can have this difficulty, but from what I have experienced, it is more prevalent in women. There were times as a teenager and young woman when

I was screaming NO inside, but the word would not come out.

My father was a good man, but a weak father figure. Thus, I never learned how to set my boundaries and maybe only twice in my life heard him speak the words "I love you." Because of my inability to say "no" and my longing for a father to express love for me, and tell me what to do, I looked outside of the home for what I wanted from my father. What I found were men who pretended to care and were good at telling me what to do, but not for the sake of my higher good. At age 16 I ended up being sexually manipulated and abused as one man made himself my pimp. I encountered men who you would expect to be a father figure, who instead contributed to my manipulation and exploitation

As a result of this phase, I became very promiscuous. This experience was something I kept a secret for many years. Like most abuse victims, I blamed myself and thought everyone was better than me. I carried the shame and guilt for 27 years before I acknowledged that I had actually been a victim, and was finally able to speak about what had taken place during those teen years. That was a turning point for me. It was when I was able to step fully into the healing process and restore my self-love and inner power.

It's one thing to *be* a victim, but as time passes, one must gain perspective. To heal, one eventually needs to stop *playing* the victim. Mine is but one of millions of stories. I am long since past the pain. My wounds are healed and I now stand strong in my Divine Feminine power of self love and nurturing. I embrace the wisdom I received from my experience. Because of this, I can serve others and help them heal their wounds. With my gifts as a healer, coach and facilitator, I help others recognize the illusion of their fear, guilt, and shame around sexuality. As they do this, they can step into their power and see the beautiful Divine being they truly are.

The fact is, we as a society need to face reality about the way children are raised and taught about their bodies. The reason there is so much promiscuity among the youth is because there is so little guidance. Young girls need a strong father figure in their lives; one who freely expresses their love and fatherly affection; one who teaches them how to say "no," and that "no" is a complete sentence; one who teaches them how to fully honor the magnificence of who they are and see it in others. As daughters are raised with this truth, they will expect to be honored by the boys and men they spend their time with, and settle for nothing less.

My story is very mild compared to most and all it takes to shift the statistics is for the youth to have strong role models and guidance. The first sexual experience most young girls have is with a young boy. How can he possibly teach her anything about her sexuality when he's still trying to figure out his own? Why do we shy away from talking openly about our sexuality and our yonis and our lingams to our youth? Our bodies are created so beautifully and are intended for pleasure. We know the youth are going to experience physical pleasure because of their sexuality, so why not teach them how to honor it and connect with it from a place of self love and spiritual consciousness? Why not teach them to recognize it as a Divine gift in themselves and one another? Why not explain to children how to give themselves pleasure from a place of love and spiritual connection? This way, during their first years of stimulation, they make the conscious connection of their sexual energy with their Divine spiritual body.

Belly dancing was originally only done for women, by women, to teach them about their bodies and their sexuality. It taught them how to harness their sexual energy, how to enjoy it, how to move their hips and savor it, while feeling fully honored, supported, and loved by other women at the same time. Imagine if all youth learned about their bodies and their sexuality in this manner. Imagine the difference it would make in our consciousness as a society. We have a responsibility to our children. Women can prepare their daughters much more powerfully once they have healed and reclaimed this part of themselves. Men can prepare their sons so much more powerfully as they also make that connection with themselves. Imagine the shift in how well grounded, aligned and wise, the youth would be, and how much healthier their relationships would be, if the teachings of Sacred Sexuality were passed down from mother to daughter and from father to son.

Men and women think and feel differently with regard to sex. Men become emotionally aroused through sexual arousal. Women become sexually aroused through emotional arousal. That is why all girls, no matter how promiscuous they are, are really just crying out to be loved. A boy and man's body is programmed differently with regards to sex. Once a boy hits puberty, sex is a constant part of his thought process. It's like us walking by the ice cream section in a grocery store. "Oooh, ice cream." For men, it's "oooh breasts… sex." It's the same kind of "passing stimulation" thought process. For women, sexuality is connected to our emotional center. We cannot disconnect the two. For those who appear to, they have most likely been cut off from love in the past and, as a protective device, pretend that love doesn't matter. I guarantee that, at their core, these women, are wounded girls longing to be loved. It's just the way we are wired. Emotions and sex are connected. You create wise boys when you teach them this.

A conscious boy or man is one who can look at a beautiful girl or woman, admire her beauty, and honor her and respect her as a Divine being rather than think, "I'd like to have that." The thoughts of "I want that," or, "I'd like to have that" are natural primal masculine thoughts. As a boy and a man becomes more conscious, they will still have this desire. They can still get the girl. The difference is in the way they treat the girl or woman, how they honor her, and how they express their respect for her. Teach your sons and nephews to be this kind of a man, and you will have guided them to be a man which all women will be drawn to. David Deida's book, *The Way of the Superior Man* is an excellent guide for becoming such a man.

If your woman is having trouble opening up to you sexually, understand that wounds around sexual energy run deep. She may have had an abusive experience in this lifetime or hold subconscious memories of her ancestors experiences. Men have not had it easy through history either. You have also been victimized by wounds of the feminine. As a boy, you may have had a wounded mother. You were expected to know instinctively how to be good lovers. Why not teach boys to honor their future sexual partners, and the importance of giving first? Teach boys to connect and acknowledge that the girls and women they have sexual relations with, no matter how brief the encounter, are Divine beings, just like themselves. Why not teach girls how to honor themselves by only sharing with those who honor them? Once this happens, our youth will experience sexuality as intended. Their relationships will be much richer and healthier for it. Until this takes place, we will have a weak link in our society.

Be gentle with one another. Learn to communicate and teach each other how to be fully present. A woman may be afraid to tell her man if the sex is not as fulfilling as it could be. She would rather be less fulfilled for years than risk hurting her man's feelings. Women don't fake orgasms to be dishonest. It's all a part of our nurturing nature. It's backwards I know, but many women fear that if they give directions in bed, their lovers will feel incompetent. It's because of this myth that men are supposed to instinctively know what to do. When we practice clear communication in a loving manner, we show up as better lovers for one another.

Most women want to have sex with a man because he has emotionally aroused her. For us, it's all about the connection. The brain is a wonderful stimulant. Humor is very sexy. A man who can make a woman laugh is off to a great start. Once we feel seen, heard, safe, and beautiful in the eyes of the man we are with, we feel connected. The more connected we feel, the more we will want to be sexual with him.

In my private sessions, I have coached many men who said that they wanted to learn to perform better in bed. Being a good lover is not about performance. It's about connection. It's a about being present with your woman. Pay attention to her body language, to the shift in her breath. Feel her. Think of the movie "Avatar" when the Navi connect their hair to the animals and the tree to make the bond. Make the bond with your woman and help her open up and communicate with you more freely. Look into her eyes and ask her questions if you are still not sure, such as, "is this the right pressure? Would you like it softer? Would you like it slower?" One thing you do want to avoid, however, is coaxing your woman to orgasm. Many men make this mistake and in the heat of the moment by saying, "cum for me." This may work for some. But for most women, it will have the opposite effect. It will interfere with their woman's ability to let go. Female orgasms do not take place by coaxing. A woman needs to feel like she is being savored and that time is no issue. Deep connection is what contributes to her ability to completely relax and let go.

The deeper, more intimate work I do with my clients includes teaching Sacred Sexuality, which is consciously acknowledging and honoring the integral connection of our sexual energy to Divine Source. It is the integral weaving of the sexual to the spiritual. I help them make this connection. I also guide them to open up the path of honest, truthful and open communication. I lead them to see in one another what they may have forgotten, and to come back to that place of awe which they had when they first fell in love. When this takes place, they can go to a deeper place of connection, honesty, and sexual pleasure.

You can help yourself heal the painful wounds of the feminine by fully honoring your woman. Maybe you have mother wounds, or wounds created from a previous relationship. When you honor the Divine Feminine in your partner, you honor the feminine within yourself. Through this process, you heal your own wounds as you help her heal hers. Just as I was writing this very section, I magically received an email in great harmony with this point. It's a long quote, but one which I feel is fitting. It was written by a man named Arjuna Ardagh. You can find him on Twitter. He speaks of the layers of a woman's heart and compares them to a series of walls. Here is what he says:

"The very essence of every woman's heart is the peak of wisdom, the peak of inspiration, the peak of sexual desirability, the peak of soothing, healing love The peak of everything. But it's protected, for good reason, by a series of concentric walls To move inwardly from one wall to the next requires that you intensify your capacity to devotion, and as you do so, you are rewarded with Grace. This is not something you can negotiate verbally with a woman. She doesn't even know consciously how to open those gates herself. They are opened magically and invisibly by the keys of worship. If you stand on the outside of the outermost wall, all you have available to you, like many other unfortunate men, is pornography. For $1.99 a minute, you can see her breasts, maybe her vagina, and you can stimulate yourself in a sad longing for deeper love.

Step through another gate, and she will show you her outer gift-wrapping. She'll look at you with a certain twinkle in her eye. She'll answer your questions coyly. She'll give you just the faintest hint that there is more available.

Step through another gate with your commitment, with your attention, with the small seedlings of devotion, and she'll open her heart to you more. She'll share with you her insecurities, the way that she's been hurt, her deepest longings. Some men will back away at this point. They realize that the price they must pay to go deeper is more than they are willing to give. They start to feel a responsibility. But for those few who step though another gate, they come to discover her loyalty, her willingness to stick with you no matter what, her willingness to raise your children, stick up for you in conversation, and, if you are lucky, even pick up your dirty socks now and then. And so it goes on. You've got the gist by now.

Somewhere around the second wall from the center, she casts the veils of her personality aside, and shows you that she is both a human being and also a portal into something much greater than that. She shows you a wrath that is not hers, but all women's. She shows you a patience that is also universal. She shows you her wisdom. At this point you start to experience the archetypes of women, who have been portrayed as goddesses and mythological figures in every tradition.

Then, at the very center, in the innermost temple itself, all the layers of your devotion are flooded with reward all at once. You discover the very essence of the feminine, and in a strange way that is not exactly romantic, but profoundly sacred all the same, you realize that you could have got here with any woman if you had just been willing to pass through all the layers of initiation. Any woman is every woman, and every woman is any woman at the same time. When you love a woman completely, at the very essence of her being, this is the one divine feminine flame. It is what has made every woman in history beautiful. It's the flame behind the Mona Lisa, and Dante's Beatrice, and yes, also Penelope Cruz and Heidi Klum. You discover the magic ingredient which has lead every man to fall in love with a woman.

When you learn how to pay attention to the essence of the feminine in this way, you fall to the floor in full body prostration, tears soaking your cheeks and clothes, and you wonder how you could have ever taken Her, in all of Her forms, for granted even for a second."

Thank you, Arjuna Ardagh. He then goes on to share how to worship your woman. I personally prefer the word "cherish." He speaks of how to do so through words of praise, just as I suggested in earlier sections of this book; by complimenting her on her scent, her beauty, the sound of her voice, the beautiful curve of her breast. The more you give to her in this way, and cherish her, the more you heal the wounds in both her and yourself. The more you will feel the Divine Feminine- her love, her nurturing- from deep inside come out and pour onto you. The more you will be her hero. The more she will blossom and want to open herself up to love with you.

"Love is the cure, for your pain will keep giving birth to more pain until your eyes constantly exhale love as effortlessly as your body yields its scent."

- Rumi

Ecstasy

Releasing

There is a posture in Sacred Tantric Sexuality called Yab-Yum. Sitting in this posture will help you make a deep soul connection and draw the sexual energy up your body more effectively. By drawing the sexual energy up your body, you will be able to prolong orgasm and last much longer during sexual intercourse. It will also leave you feeling highly energized after orgasm, rather than depleted and tired.

This practice of drawing the sexual energy up the body is perfect in assisting men with premature ejaculation issues. So often during the sexual act, there is a tendency to hold the breath or breathe shallow. This limits the sexual energy to your genital area. Simply by breathing this energy up your body, it will help prevent it from being dispersed through ejaculation prematurely.

Another cause of premature ejaculation can also go back to the early years of sexual experience. If this has been an issue for you, think back to when you first entered puberty. When you pleasured yourself, did you feel the need to get it over with quickly in fear that you may get caught? If so, this could be the source of your premature ejaculation. Fear of any kind can manifest itself into the physical. If this resonates with you, simply by identifying it, you can release it- no pun intended.

Take a moment to visualize yourself as that boy. Now that you are an adult, you can talk to your child self. Tell him it's ok now. He can relax and take his time as much as he wants. Let him know it's safe now. If your ejaculation became premature later in life, think back and look at what was going on with you at that time. Were you with a lover who made you feel less than for any reason? If so, they were most likely not very self loving and you were simply the object of their projection. Explore this and if you find an emotion around your sexual energy which surfaced at the same time the premature ejaculation did, bring it to the light. Send loving energy to yourself and bring conscious awareness to the fact that you can relax now.

Divine Union

Yab-Yum is Sanskrit for "Father-Mother," denoting the perfect balance between physical and spiritual, male and female. It represents the divine strength of creation. The most common way to assume this posture is for the man to sit in the lotus position with the woman on his lap. Comfort is important here, so if you are not flexible enough to do that, you can sit with your legs straight out with pillows supporting, and you can use a support for your back, such as a headboard or you can even do this sitting in a chair. Before she sits on your lap, start connecting by facing one another with your knees touching.

Look deep inside your beloved and let her feel your presence. Now feel the unconditional love of God Source energy and invite this energy to be present as you share in this Divine Union. This is an important step. So often lovers forget or don't think to invite Source to the party. Sexual energy is very powerful. Energy attracts energy. If you do not consciously invite the energy of love and light, you leave yourself vulnerable to having unwanted energy enter into your realm. This can be especially true after a couple has been together for a long time. As love making feels more familiar, distractions can more easily enter into the experience, even though your love can be quite strong, allowing distractions to enter the love making experience weaken the energy. By taking a moment to align in this way, you empower the experience in the most beautiful way.

To further deepen the experience, show her beauty to her through your eyes. The left eye is the side we receive with. It is our vulnerable side, and it is easier to see into the soul of another through this eye. In Tantric practice, eye gazing is done through the left eye. You can feel the difference. Try it. Gaze into one another's left eye, while taking deep, relaxed breaths together. Then try it with the right eye. It will not feel as connected. Continue with this left eye gazing and synchronize your breath together, inhaling and exhaling at the same time. If one of you feels the urge to make a joke of it- making faces or giggling- your ego is avoiding a deeper connection. Stay with it. You still want it to be playful and fun. Just notice if it's playful laughter or your ego mind trying to distract you from the connection. Remember, your breath is what keeps the energy- the spirit in your body. This practice of eye gazing and feeling one another's breath merges your spirits together. Now place your hand over one another's heart to enhance the connection and help the heart connect to the sexual energy.

If sexual intimacy has not been a part of your relationship for a while, the simple practice of eye gazing and breathing together will be a beautiful way to reestablish your connection. As you do this, verbalize at least three things you appreciate about each another as love partners. If she needs time to open up, just stay with the breathing and the eye contact without the sexual activation. The more you help her open up her heart and connect with her in this way, the easier it will be for her to open up and engage in sexual play. Continue to connect with her left eye. See if you sense her inviting you to take your connection further. Then ask, "May I touch your neck?" If her answer is an immediate eye contact "yes," then gently caress and touch her neck while still looking into her left eye. Continue in this way, always asking permission to touch her in a new place. If she pauses when she answers, the answer is "no;" if she says maybe, the answer is "no." Only a direct eye contact "yes" means yes. So often a woman will agree to something to make her man happy when inside she feels she is not quite ready.

As your energy gets activated and she feels ready, your Goddess can sit on top of you with her legs wrapped around you. This experience can be powerful with or without penetration, however most couples find penetration more fun. Your choice. Now you're now ready to take it up a notch. Both of you visualize and feel your breath moving upward through your body as you gently rotate your pelvises together. Face the palms of your hands toward the back of one another, starting at the base of the spine, then each of you move your hands in an upward motion to assist the movement of the sexual energy up the body. This can be done in a gentle caressing motion. As this becomes a natural rhythm, then start contracting your PC muscle on the inhale.

This will also activate your sexual energy and help intensify the experience. Your PC muscle (pubococcygeus), is the same one you would squeeze to stop yourself from going pee. Imagine your PC muscle actually drawing the sexual energy up your body. Maintain your eye contact to one another throughout this process. As you feel your beloved fully in her feminine and opening to you, breathe in her essence and savor this moment completely. Feel your hearts opening together as you continue to breathe together. Gaze into one another's eyes and feel the love of Divine Source as you share in this bliss.

The deeper you go with this breath work and simple eye gazing practice, the more arousing it can become. As you become more experienced, it is actually possible to have an orgasm without even touching yourself or one another, just from eye contact, breathing and with the help of the PC muscle,

Once the energy has really elevated, stop any pelvic movement you may be doing, place your hand on one another's heart and now as you exhale, she inhales. When you exhale, send your sexual energy out through your lingam into her yoni. She receives your energy through her inhale, drawing the sexual energy up through the center of her body to her heart. Then she exhales her love energy into your heart center. You inhale, drawing this energy down through the center of your body, back to your lingam. Keep circulating the energy in this way. This is a magical and powerful process. Continue breathing out through your lingam, into her yoni. She keeps breathing out through her heart into your heart. Continue the process as long as you are able to sustain it. Have fun with it. Playfulness activates a sense of joy. When we are joyful, we are in direct alignment with who we truly are as a Divine Source energy being.

She will invite you in through your initiation, and the more you open up and give to her, the more she will open up and give back. The more deeply you see her, the more she will feel you. The amount of giving and surrender she gives to you is measured by the degree of giving and surrender you give to her. This is Sacred Tantric Sexuality; intertwining your spiritual essence and sexual energy in deep connection, breathing one another in fully and completely. It is the merging of your masculine and feminine essence as you fully savor every moment, every breath, every fragment of one another. It is about staying fully present, in every second. She may cry tears of love-filled emotion as you perform this practice with her. Receive that, and don't be afraid to let go and cry with her. This can then quickly shift to laughter from sheer joy in the depth of what you feel at this moment. Laughter is good. It's an essential element to maintaining a playful partnership.

If you'd like to stop reading and get busy experiencing this juicy energy with your beloved, I have a special gift offering for you. I created an audio for readers only which you can download right now and have my voice guide you through this Sacred connection process. So put down the book and go log in at: www.ThePlayfulPartnershipBook.com to receive your audio gift, titled, *Divine Union*. It's much easier to do the breath work and gaze into the eyes of your beloved with my voice guiding you through the process, rather than reading instructions. After a few times with my guidance, you will feel the flow and be able to continue the practice on your own. I am confident this practice will intensify the beautiful love you already share and add a whole new Divine dimension to your love making.

As you caress and kiss your woman, look upon her body as if you are seeing her for the very first time. Explore every crevice. Feel her softness. Drink in her beauty. Make eye contact with her often. Give to her and fill her up fully before receiving orgasm for yourself. Oral sex is a favorite way to receive among many women. I know men love it too. The secret to receiving great oral sex is to first give it slowly and completely to your woman. She is the receptor. She responds to what she is given. As you fill her up, she will feel inspired to give back in the same way she received. Once she has reached the peak of her pleasure, do not let her reciprocate right away. Hold her and let the energy vibrate through her body. Allow her to savor and stay with her orgasm to receive the fullness of it.

Remember, this beautiful sexual energy is our life force. Our bodies were created perfectly as fully intended in all their deliciousness. As we fully connect our sexual energy to that of our heart center and to Source, and as we breathe it throughout our bodies, we experience sexual energy in its most potent form.

We are also human and have an integral connection to this earthly realm. This is why it is healthy to weave the raw energy of your primal force with tenderness. Hold nothing back; give her all of you. I know sometimes letting go of everything in this vulnerable state can even feel fearful. That part of you which needs to be in control may feel the need to hold on to something. Let it go- all of it. Offer yourself to her completely. Let the warmth and openness of her heart carry you and drink you in.

As she is fully in her feminine essence in this moment, she is at her most powerful. The Divine Feminine is love, compassion, nurturing and inspiration. She will carry you now. Breathe this life force throughout your entire body and continue to connect with her through eye contact. Her radiance is at its most beautiful in this moment. Breathe it in. See the beauty and perfection which is you reflected back through her eyes. This is Divine Union. This is why you do the work you do; to breathe, live, play, laugh, have fun, share the gift of you, to make love, and have the freedom to experience Divine ecstasy.

Take this awareness into all aspects of your life. When you eat a piece of fruit, feel the sensuality of it. Savor the juice and acknowledge the miracle that this sweet nectar exists for us to enjoy and indulge in. Feel the richness which Mother Earth has to offer all around us; the lushness of a rain forest, the intensity of a torrential rain, the softness and incredible beauty of spring flowers, the nurturing heat of the summer sun. Make love to life as if it were a woman and your life will be all the richer for it. Life is ecstasy, if we just open our eyes and see it and breathe it in. Remember why we came to this planet. Work to live, don't live to work.

It's incredible how much we as a society have disconnected both sex and money from the Divine. No wonder the planet is in disarray. Remember, it's you who makes the choice for money to carry the energy of love. You can also channel your love for one another to empower the financial abundance in your life. The sexual energy is our creative force. Because of the sexual energy, we go from being a nonphysical spiritual being and manifest into a physical spiritual being. That's creation at its finest. With the awareness that the sexual is our creative force, we can actually channel the energy generated as we make love to help transform our dreams to reality, including attracting greater financial wealth.

Try this: as you begin your romantic evening together, sit looking into one another's eyes. Speak out loud about the dreams you share, the abundance you desire, and express appreciation for the gifts you both contribute toward making it happen. You're not getting into business talk here. You're simply acknowledging your individual gifts. Clearly state everything you are grateful for and happy for in your life right now. Then visualize for a moment where you desire your lives to evolve to. Feel the joy of what it is like to be living this dream as though it's already here, now, in present time.

Now hold this joy and take it into your love making. As your sexual energy peaks and your love flows, feel your lives complete with abundance. Feel your bodies healthy, your love deepening and prosperity flowing. Your creative force is in its most powerful state when you make love; the deeper your connection to your love and to Source, and the more you connect with the sheer joy of the moment, the more powerful your creative force becomes. This exercise of appreciation and visualization is very powerful to practice as you move into making love with one another. It is the most beautiful manifestation fuel you can share together. Now this is a playful partnership!

"When you feel good, everything around you is good. When everything around you is great, everything makes you happy. You are loving everything that is around you, because you are loving yourself. Because you like the way you are. Because you are content with you. Because you are happy with your life...
...You are at peace, and you are happy. You live in that state of bliss where everything is so wonderful, and everything is so beautiful. In that state of bliss you are making love all the time with everything you perceive."

- Don Miguel Ruiz, "The Four Agreements"

"The best day of your life is the one on which you decide your life is your own. No apologies or excuses. No one to lean on, rely on, or blame. The gift is yours – it is an amazing journey – and you alone are responsible for the quality of it. This is the day your life really begins."

- Bob Moawad, author

Sweet Dreams

Thank you for reading my words. I hope they have provided you with enough insight to make a difference in your life. If this book makes even a small contribution to helping you keep greater harmony in your business and maintain passion in your playtime, then my work is done. It has been an honor and a blessing to share. I would love to hear from you and receive any feedback you feel inspired to offer, through my book site: ThePlayfulPartnershipBook.com

If you enjoyed this book, then pass it on to your woman. It's intended for her as well. Gift your single friends with a copy. It will be incredible preparation for their next relationship. I highly recommend you purchase David Dieda's, "The Way of the Superior Man." You've seen many of his quotes in this book. I suggest it be every man's bible to better understanding, living with, and loving women. If you enjoyed the quotes, you will love the book. I also recommend "It's a Guy Thing" by David Dieda as a great read for your beloved, to better understand where you are coming from.

John Gray is also a highly respected author and a wonderful source of wisdom to continue bringing clarity to the mysteries of the masculine and feminine.

I'd like to think my feminine, loving, and sometimes bold perspective gave you a new outlook on how to live and work in greater harmony with your beloved.

If you or someone you know is looking for a keynote speaker at their next event, I thank you for your recommendation. In addition to working with couples, I offer an effective and fun presentation on leadership and team in the work place, through better understanding of the power source of the

Masculine and Feminine, and how to weave them together for maximum productivity and harmony in the work place.

If you would like to go into more depth on the information offered in this book, I would love to serve you in one of my coaching programs, guaranteed to create greater success in your business and more bliss at home. When you go to my main website: www.ThePlayfulPartnership.com, visit my *Coaching* page. There you will find details on the *Beloveds in Business Series.* You have the choice of working with me to help you create greater harmony in your business, deepen your intimacy, or both. I can help you and your beloved create an expansive new relationship with money, get more clients and build a lucrative internet presence.

My intimacy coaching will help you deepen the connection you already have, turn up the heat in your love and create blissful expansion. If you would like to create an immediate shift in your romantic relationship, I recommend my weekend retreat which can be done virtually or in person working directly with me in a beautiful exotic setting.

You can create the freedom you've always dreamed of (or turn up the heat in your relationship) and use that energy to fuel the business. So, if you're ready to make more money and have more blissful sex with your beloved, I look forward to connecting with you at ThePlayfulPartnership.com and supporting you along your journey.

It is so important for women to gather with other sister women from a place of love and support, and equally as important for men to gather with their brothers from a place of high consciousness and enlightenment. The husband of Anyaa McAndrew who I spoke about in the section titled, "Her-story" is brilliant on facilitating conscious events and connections for men. He is also a dear friend. His name is Gary Stamper. He can be found at GaryStamper.com. Gary is a Divine Masculine man and is who I choose to work with when creating couples retreats.

We all have the ability to make our dreams come true. Sometimes we're just too close to our own reality, and we need a little guidance along the way. Just make sure you take action, and find the help you need so you and your beloved can create a life of ultimate abundance and intimate ecstasy.

My wish is for the both of you to manifest sweet dreams into a sweet reality. Blessings to you both.

53859520R00109

Made in the USA
San Bernardino, CA
30 September 2017